MW01165562

No More Business as Usual: The Church Then & Now

Straight Talk for this Generation of Church-goers

by

Walter Gibson

Bloomington, IN

authorHOUSE™

Milton Keynes, UK

AuthorHouse™
1663 Liberty Drive, Suite 200
Bloomington, IN 47403
www.authorhouse.com
Phone: 1-800-839-8640

AuthorHouse™ UK Ltd.
500 Avebury Boulevard
Central Milton Keynes, MK9 2BE
www.authorhouse.co.uk
Phone: 08001974150

This book is a work of non-fiction. Unless otherwise noted, the author and the publisher make no explicit guarantees as to the accuracy of the information contained in this book and in some cases, names of people and places have been altered to protect their privacy.

First published by AuthorHouse 5/25/2006

ISBN: 1-4208-8088-8 (sc)

Printed in the United States of America
Bloomington, Indiana

This book is printed on acid-free paper.

Acknowledgements

I give thanks to my wife Tarsha and my boys Cameron and Christian for encouraging me. Thanks to my parents Walter & Opal Gibson for raising me to love God and to always put him first. Thanks to Pastor Willie Jones and the New Mt. Calvary Baptist Church family. I have learned so much from you all and the half has yet to be told! I express my sincere gratitude to the family of the late Janice Gibson, who pushed me out of my comfort zone to put my thoughts into print.

Special thanks to the Sharp family, Barbara Owens, Pam Pointer, Nather Simsons, the Burkley family, the Hernandez family, and the Carpenters. Thanks for making this dream a reality! Praise God, for all the things He has done!

Table of Contents

Introduction

The church. Who is it? What is it? From where did it come? How did it look in the beginning? How does it look now? What was its original purpose? What is its purpose today? Wow! Got you thinking now, right?

The term church has taken on different meanings over the years. In some circles when you say church, it means a building. There are so many church buildings around today and depending on what block you are on, you will see at least three or four within a few yards of one another. If we view the church as a physical building made of wood, brick and steel where people come together and hear a song and a sermon, then that is not the church Jesus Christ came to set up. We can conclude that buildings never have and never will change people. People get excited for a while when a new building is erected, but that excitement rarely lasts and soon the building becomes old and public opinion turns to the acquisition of another building.

To others the term church describes what goes on inside the building. The singing, the preaching, and the programs whatever form they may take is called church. From this view of the term we hear the phrase, "we had some good church today". It is not uncommon to catch a comedian mocking what is known as "having church". From the tones and gyrations of the preacher to the emotional outburst of the congregants, the world considers what is expressed on Sunday mornings as being church. Even in the television shows, the church only appears when someone gets married or someone dies. If this is what the world believes the church to be, evidently the church is off track and we must get back on track. In this sense of the word church is a systematic way of uplifting a group of people for a specified period of time, (usually at the 11 o'clock hour on Sunday morning), where they are emotionally stirred to the point of tears and sorrow for the things they have done. People choose what church they will attend based on how effective a church can have church. Don't seek a commitment from them and don't expect them to get involved in the ministry. Their main concern is having church. Being entertained is their goal.

In the face of being different things to different people, the church has accomplished some extraordinary things. The church has grown in terms of numbers and building sizes. From wooden buildings that could hold no more than a few hundred people to mega churches with the capacity to hold thousands. No longer is the church simply a place of worship but it has become a center for economic re-development. The church is making available jobs for people who were once down and out, and what at one time had been considered the most segregated hour in this country (Sunday worship) is being transformed as denominational walls and cultural barriers are coming down. Different nationalities and races are beginning to worship God together in spirit and in truth.

What at one time seemed impossible is becoming the norm. The church of the 21st century is positioned in a spot where God will receive all the glory and millions will be saved. People are looking for answers to life's most critical questions. The bottom line is people want to know how to experience peace in a world full of turmoil and confusion.

It was made evident after September 11, 2001 that we had not forgotten God. Those who had not been to church for years filled sanctuaries all over this nation seeking real answers to help ease their troubled minds in that time of crises. When it is all said and done, deep down inside of us we know that true peace, love, joy, and happiness only comes from God. God is still calling the church to be the vehicle that administers real answers to life's most difficult questions and to be the place where all people can experience God in a real and personal way.

However, before we can realize the full measure of what God has in store for us and the impact we are to make in the world, we must get back to the true business of the church. We must agree on what this word church really means. Is it a system? Is it a building? Is it an economic machine?

Having large memberships is fine, but that is not what the church is. Having a nice building is fine, but this is not what the church is. Having church owned businesses is fine, but this is not what the church is. Having the best choir around is not the church nor is having a great preacher/pastor.

It is evident as we look at the multi-million dollar budgets of churches today that the church in many circles has become big business. Don't get me wrong, without funds the church cannot do ministry to the extent it would like, but when the motivation behind bringing in finances has nothing to do with bringing glory to God and reaching the lost, then the church is no longer the house of prayer but a den of thieves (Mark 11: 15-18).

Once I was looking through some old pictures at my parent's house with my youngest son Christian who was 4 years old at the time. As I strolled down memory lane from pre-school to elementary, from elementary to middle school, from middle school to high school, what joy I felt in my soul. To see where God had brought me from was amazing. I thought about what my dreams were at the particular times those pictures were taken. Many of the things I dreamed about as a child didn't come to pass because of decisions made to go in another direction. Not only that in other cases as I got older, I was not willing to do what it took to make my dreams reality. How often have you known what it took to reach a destination but obstacles, pretty scenery and detours got you off track? When we get off track, before we know it we find ourselves on a different road than the one we started on and our original goal and mission have been altered.

As I looked at the pictures, I saw myself. From my point of view, I had not changed that much, although I had more hair back then and was about 40 pounds lighter. I remember thinking those were the good old days. No bills. No worries. No real responsibility. If I could do it all over again! Oh the joy I felt inside. However, that feeling didn't last long. My time of reflection was interrupted as I pointed to a middle school football picture of myself. As Christian looked at the picture, he glanced at me, then back at the picture. With a look of confusion on his little innocent face, he mouthed these words, "You don't look like him on the picture."

"What do you mean?"

"That's not you daddy. That's somebody else."

What happens when we change to a point that what we once were cannot be seen in what we have become? For the next three minutes, I sat on the couch with my four year old son trying to convince him that the little boy on the picture wearing the number thirty was in fact his daddy, but regardless of what I said, he continuously said, "You don't look like him on the picture."

It was not until a few months later the words of my son hit me like a ton of bricks- "You don't look like him on the picture." Only this time it was not the picture of a seventh grade football player wearing the number 30 that the words were being addressed to. It was not the voice of an innocent four-year old looking at a picture of his dad some 20 years earlier, but the gentle whisper of the Holy Spirit saying church of the 21st century, you don't look like the original!

Yes, change is inevitable and without it growth is impossible. However, with change, certain values and foundational principles must remain intact because if they don't, in the process of change what once was ceases to exist.

Pictures are powerful tools. They show us our good traits, they help us to remember what was once upon a time and they show us how much we have changed. All of us at one point or another has looked back at some old picture with the thought if I could get back to that size, or if I could wear my hair like that again, or if I had that six pack again (ripples in the stomach, you know what I mean!). As powerful as a picture of your physical body may be to inspire you to make a change in your current look or to simply get back to where you once were, there is not a more powerful picture of the church than Acts 2. In this wonderful picture, we see qualities that every good church should possess.

What is the church? Who is it? From where did it come? How did it originally look? How does it look now?

Chapter 1

A Great Beginning

They were a small band of eleven men. One had been a doubter. Another denied that he even knew the man. Still others vanished from the scene. Yet it was to this group of eleven men that Jesus commissioned to carry on his work and take the gospel to the whole world (Matthew 28:16). Without television, airplanes, telephones, automobiles, or even UPS, these eleven men, along with a growing constituency, went from house to house, from door to door, from city to city spreading the gospel message.

In a world today where technological advances are being made daily, it seems sharing the gospel message is one of the hardest things to involve congregations in. There are airplanes that can get people to other parts of the world in a matter of hours as opposed to the days and even months of travel on dusty roads and ships the early Christians endured to spread the gospel to other cities and regions.

The resources available to assist in the fulfilling of this commission are inexhaustible. Numerous books have been written and study guides compiled. "How to" videos have been produced along with everything a person needs to effectively share the gospel. Yet that fire that burned in the hearts of the original disciples and spread to the hearts of the early church to evangelize the lost is not as hot in the church today.

If the gospel is to spread today, it must be done from house to house, door to door, city to city, at coffee breaks, grocery stores, shopping malls, recreation centers and churches. The fire that burned in the heart of the early church must be rekindled in the hearts of today's church.

First and last words

First and last words are very important. They give insight into the very heart and desire of the individual who spoke them. In Mark's gospel, the first words Jesus spoke to two potential disciples, Simon Peter and Andrew were "follow me and I will make you fishers of men" (Mark 1:17). First words are very important.

Just as first words are important, last words are important as well and maybe even more so. When people are aware that the words being spoken may be the individual's last words, they listen closely. Last words convey the person's hearts desire. Last words convey to the listener what the speaker wants to be carried on after he/she has exited the stage of life. Jesus' last words were these:

> *But you will receive power when the Holy Ghost has come upon you; and you shall be my witnesses both in Jerusalem, and Judea and Samaria, and even to the remotest part of the earth (Acts 1:8).*

Throughout scripture, the purpose of God's people in the Old Testament and the church in the New Testament was to bring people into a right relationship with the true and living God. It is not a choice, but a command. Jesus chose his words carefully. The statement that those who choose to follow him will become fishers of men gives insight into how Jesus intends for the Christian church today to win men, women, boys and girls to him. The allegory of becoming fishers of men conveys a word picture-job description for the church.

Followers of Jesus Christ have been labeled with a few names. We are salt in Matthew 5:13. We are light in Matthew 5:14. We are a royal priesthood in 1 Peter 2:9. We are fishers of men in Mark 1:17. If we live the lifestyle conveyed by these designations, those who are not in the family of God will look upon us and see that there is something we have that they need. Christians must be loving, patient, understanding, always willing to lend a helping hand, giving, and always ready to give an answer for the hope that is within us (1 Peter 3:15).

The church has done a good job in several areas of worship and service to God. The giving of money within the church as an act of worship is up as is evident by the great buildings that are being erected all over the world. Praise has been elevated to another level as people are lifting their hands and voices in praise despite the opinions of those who say, "it doesn't take all that". The church has more knowledge of the Word of God than any other time in history. There are more doctors of the word, workshops, conferences and schools to assist in spiritual growth. All of these things are wonderful, but one aspect of worship has been placed on the back burner and that is holy living. We will discuss the importance of holy living later because without it, the church is a weak and irrelevant part of society.

As children we are taught to share what we have with others. Daily we encounter individuals on the highways and by-ways of life who are not blessed to know what we know nor have what we have. They are starving physically. The things many Christians take for granted such as food, shelter, clothes, jobs, stable relationships and peace of mind, are not readily available to all. In a picture perfect world, one would wish all people could enjoy these liberties. However, the truth of the matter is many are going without.

In 2 Corinthians 5:20, Paul states the purpose of the church.

> *Therefore, we are ambassadors for Christ, as though God were entreating through us; we beg you on behalf of Christ, be reconciled to God.*

We will discuss the role of an ambassador in a later chapter as well, however, the Christian message to the world is simple and plain; be reconciled to God. In spreading this message, we must be in lifestyle what we profess with our mouths and display on Sunday mornings. When we come together for our corporate worship experiences, we are only filling up to go back into the world as royal priests, light, and salt. Millions attend Sunday morning worship services, mid-week bible classes and so on, so why is there so much darkness in the world? I would suggest that our message to the world is not accompanied by holy living. Our message to the world, although unintentional, is do as we sing, do as we preach and teach, but don't do as we do. We must change!

It Started With Twelve

What a time it must have been during those forty days after the resurrection of Jesus; from a period of confusion to times of refreshing and a new commitment; from a period of fear to a life of boldness and from a period of disharmony to a time of unity. He spoke to them. He ate with them. He taught them, laughed with them, and inspired them. What a glorious time that must have been! But suddenly, Jesus was leaving, going back to the Father.

Gazing into the sky, they watched as he departed. The faithful few had come to accept the fact that the world would never be the same as they watched Jesus, their friend, their teacher, their brother, Mary's baby, and their Lord ascend into the clouds to take His rightful place at the right hand of the Father. What a turn around! Over a month ago it appeared that their hope was lost as they watched Jesus die on the cross. They had watched from a distance, fearful of what men would say or do to them, as he carried His cross to Calvary. His beaten and bruised body on display for all to see as he, the Lamb of God made his way to the altar of sacrifice. Nailed to the cross, with a crown of thorns atop his head, he completed his mission.

> *Knowing that all things had already been accomplished, in order that the scripture might be fulfilled, said, "I am thirsty." A jar full of sour wine was standing there; so they put a sponge full of sour wine upon a branch of hyssop, and brought it up to His mouth. When Jesus therefore had received the sour wine, He said, "It is finished!" And He bowed His head, and gave up His spirit (John 19:28-30).*

His work of reconciling man back to the Father was complete. He had come to show us the way. While here He changed lives through His dedication to the will of the Father. He died on the cross between two thieves for the sins of the world but glory to God, Jesus rose with victory forever. He not only redeemed us in His death, but he gave us new courage to live for Him; for even if we lose our lives for Him, we will get up again just as He did. His followers were totally convinced that Jesus was who He claimed to be. He was the Son of God. The time had finally come to build the body of Christ.

When we are a part of something we have passion for or that we have had some part in building, we have a tendency to want to claim ownership of it. To feel a sense of ownership is good to a certain extent. Ownership drives us to support the idea or institution we have claimed ownership of. When we are willing to share and allow others to take part in what we own, that is a good thing. On the other hand, when we hold on to things we assert ownership of to the point we cannot relinquish it to someone else to take it to another level, then we have a problem.

The church has found itself in a situation where the old does not want to make way for the new. Many who have been in the church for years do not want to relinquish positions, power, authority, and even seats because they believe the church belongs to them and they are not going anywhere. This is the reason why so many churches are not growing in the way that God wants them to. They choose to do ministry the same way they did it fifty years ago and refuse to listen to the new ways the current generation seeks to do ministry. Jesus addressed this issue in Matthew 9:16-17.

> *But no one puts a patch of unshrunk cloth on an old garment; for the patch pulls away from the garment, and a worse tear results. Nor do men put new wine into old wineskins; otherwise the wineskins burst, and the wine pours out, and the wineskins are ruined; but they put new wine into fresh wineskins, and both are preserved (NAS).*

Jesus was letting the people of that day and succeeding generations know that we must strive to maintain a proper relationship between the settlers and the pioneers.

Settlers have come to a point in life where they are comfortable with the way things are. They have worked for years to get where they are and are now resting on their accomplishments. For many of the settlers, what they do is all they know. The factors they dealt with growing up shaped their view of the world and life in general. The ways they address issues is the product of their life and times. We are where we are because of them, and Jesus made that perfectly clear in this parable. He did not say the old garments and the old wineskins (settlers) were bad or useless, what he said was there is an inherent danger in trying to mix the old garments and old wineskins (settlers) with the new garments and the new wine (pioneers). What we must begin to understand is that the old ways and the new ways are a fine combination, but when one neglects the other, both suffer.

Pioneers are the "now" generation. The factors that shaped the thinking of the settlers are quite different than the pioneers. Pioneers see the world differently. The challenges of the day are different. Pioneers search for new and creative ways to handle the issues of their day. If the settlers are not willing to pass the baton to the pioneers, conflict arises and as Jesus said, the garments, patches, new wine, and old wineskins are all ruined. Are you a pioneer or a settler?

New Conditions

And of the sons of Issachar, men who understood the times, with knowledge of what Israel should do, their chiefs were two hundred; and all their kinsmen were at their command (1 Chronicles 12:32, NAS).

Times have changed. People have changed. The morals and values held by previous generations are almost extinct. With the change of morals and values comes the modification of behavior. What at one time was embarrassing has become the acceptable norm. We are seeing more teenage pregnancies. Kids are taking guns to school not to show them off, but to use them on their classmates. Kids are making bombs in their parent's garage and because their parents spend little or no time conversing with them, they have no clue of their children's doings. Men and women no longer value marriage as sacred and a life long commitment. Ease and comfort are the mainstays of the day, hard work is a thing of the past and many people have a "give me" mentality. This mentality says, "I don't have to work". I can have others take care of me and be content in letting them do so. It seems this generation has lost the conviction of the classic song, *God bless the child that's got his own.*

This Generation

This generation of churchgoers seeks to be different than their parents and grandparents. The issues confronting this generation cannot be dealt with in traditional ways. While riding in my car one afternoon listening to a Christian talk show, one of the guests on the show made this comment:

The church faces a generation which is trying to drink its way to prosperity, war its way to peace, spend its way to wealth and enjoy its way to heaven.

How true this statement is. Just talking to people hoping they will change will not get it. People in general do not value the opinions of others today as was the case years ago. It's not what you say anymore it's what you do and how you live daily.

The language of this generation is very different than that of twenty and thirty years ago. Things that meant one thing years ago have a totally different meaning today.

- A mouse was a rodent. Today it is a computer device.
- A virus was a sickness. Today it is a computer damaging program.
- A joint was a part of the body. Today it is a stick of marijuana.

The list goes on. So if things today don't mean the same as they did yesterday, then it just stands to reason that those who can speak the language and understand the times should be in the positions to do the work of ministry, their way.

Now when Jesus came into the district of Caesarea Philippi. He began asking His disciples, saying, "Who do people say that the Son of Man is?" And they said, "Some say John the Baptist; and others, Elijah; but still others, Jeremiah, or one of the prophets." He said to them, "But who do you say that I am?" And Simon Peter answered and said, "Thou art the Christ, the Son of the living God." And Jesus answered and said to him, "Blessed are you, Simon Barjona, because flesh and blood did not reveal this to you, but My Father who is in heaven. And I also say to you that you are Peter, and upon this rock I will build my church; and the gates of Hades shall not overpower it" (Matthew 16: 13-18).

Jesus said the church belonged to him. Not to Peter. Not to Thomas or any of the other disciples. Jesus said he would build his church. Those of us who are a part of the church would do well to heed the words of Jesus, "My church." Whenever someone in whom we respect highly allows us to assist them in the work they are doing, we count it a privilege and honor, and we resolve to do our very best in hope of pleasing the one whom we are working for. We must realize that Jesus has allowed us to participate in the building of his church.

> For we are God's fellow workers; you are God's field, God's building (1 Corinthians 3:9).

God gives each of us a season to be lead construction workers in His building project. While we have the physical strength and wherewithal to be effective in our work, God uses our commitment, availability and know-how to get the job done. But there is one thing that we must accept and that is accepting when the time has come to allow others to take our place in the building. We can't hog the hammer. We have to pass it on. This is not to say that people are to be thrown to the side, but we should be willing and humble enough to identify those who can take what we've done and add to it to the glory of God and the building up of the kingdom.

God expects us to build in our generation. If we try to build succeeding generations the same way we did in our generation, we run the risk of building buildings that are not equipped to handle the winds and waves of that particular generation. The winds of this generation are blowing harder than ever before and we must allow those who are fighting against the winds to use what they have experienced to build spiritual structures that will stand up against the storms.

Hebrews 11:7 speaks of Noah's faith in God to build an ark during a time when it had never rained and no rain was in sight. However, Noah believed God and obeyed.

> By faith Noah being warned by God about things not yet seen, in reverence prepared an ark for the salvation of his household.

God gave Noah specific instructions of how to build the ark because that which Noah was to build had to be strong enough to handle the storm that was at hand. God knew what the storm would bring and placed within the heart of Noah, a man who would live in and through the storm, how to build the structure that would handle the storm. I believe the Holy Spirit is molding men, women, boys and girls to be the Noahs of their generation. We must pray for them. Encourage them. Be slow to criticize their beliefs and methods as long as they are building on the sure foundation of Jesus Christ.

Can you imagine the criticism Noah must have incurred building a ship on dry ground with no evidence that it would ever be used? Why believe this ark needed to be built? Did God really tell you to build this ark?

Imagine if he would have stopped. What if he would have listened to the critics who said it doesn't take all that and you should build it with this type of wood or use this type of pitch? It is evident that Noah understood the times in which he lived and at the same time heard God's plan of how he should prepare for what was ahead. The message that Noah preached remained the same- children get ready because it's going to rain. Yes, some thought he was off base. His message was criticized. He was ostracized by the masses. But when the storm came, Noah and those who took heed to what God was saying and doing through Noah were saved.

As I sit in my study and write these words some discussions today with people have made Noah's building project and all it must have entailed come alive in me. I must be honest and say to you that I believe we are not doing enough in the church to promote holy living. We promote giving, fellowship, and commitment to inside ministries. We preach the love of God and the grace of God and that's wonderful, but we cannot continue to preach and teach these truths to the neglect of holiness.

The one thing that remains the same from building to building is that every building must be built on a firm foundation. Without a firm foundation, the building will not stand. However, driving from neighborhood to neighborhood, city to city, we see all sorts of homes and buildings with different architectural structures. It is very difficult to go downtown in any city and find two identical buildings. Even in our own neighborhoods you rarely see identical houses. Why? Because those working on a particular skyscraper or house have a particular plan they have designed based on how they want to build using the tools and resources available to them. Although every builder has as his ultimate goal to build a sturdy building, every builder will not build using the same plan, tools, or even people. The buildings may look different, but this fact still remains; each of them is still a building. The way this generation will have to handle its issues may not look the same as previous generations, but as long as its source is Jesus Christ, the package may look different, but the contents are the same.

The Saul Syndrome

We can no longer give second class service to the Supreme Builder of the house. He does not deserve anything but our best work. When I think about all the Lord has done for me, I can't help but give him my best. We must be content while it is day in our lives and work with all our heart, soul and mind. If we do this, we won't be bitter when the night time comes because we won't have any regrets. If we don't adhere to this philosophy, we subject ourselves to the Saul syndrome.

> *When the men were returning home after David had killed the Philistine, the women came out from the towns of Israel to meet King Saul with singing and dancing, with joyful songs and with tambourines and lutes. As they danced, they sang: "Saul has slain his thousands, and David his tens of thousands."" Saul was very angry; this refrain galled him. "They have credited David with tens of thousands," he thought, "but me with only thousands. What more can he get but the kingdom?" And from that time on Saul kept a jealous eye on David. (1 Samuel 18:6-9).*

The problem with staying too long, trying to work beyond our time of effectiveness, and not having a heart to allow someone else to take our place is that we make ourselves prime candidates to the evil effects of jealousy. Had Saul done everything that God told him to do he would have been content with the accolades that were now being hoisted onto David. Regret coupled with a hard heart always leads to jealousy. Saul became jealous of David because he felt David was receiving more credit than he was and that the people were beginning to like David more than him. If Saul had been content in what he had done, there would have been no room in his heart for jealousy. But because Saul knew he had disobeyed God and God had rejected him, it was easy for jealousy to take control of his thinking.

Jealousy has ruined many people and churches and destroyed the best of relationships. If we are all workers together in the building of something that does not even belong to us, there should be no jealousy. However, we know that it's there because we deal with it daily in the life of the church.

Jealousy is one of the biggest problems in the church today. Many believe that the church program will not go on without them. They are of the mindset that no one can do the job better than they can and no one deserves the spot or position but them because it belongs to them. This may sound ridiculous, but you know I am telling the truth. Let me say this. Regardless of how long you have been a member of a particular church and even if your grandfather's name is on the cornerstone, that church is not yours. Nothing in the church belongs to us. When is the last time you saw a construction worker pass by a building he/she helped construct and say, "That building belongs to me?" Just because he/she worked on the building does not give him/her any rights of ownership in the building. The same is true for the church. We are builders and not owners. No matter how much time, money, or effort we give in the building of the church, it will never belong to us. Yes, we are the builders, but we are also the church. We do not belong to ourselves, we belong to God.

When we become jealous, we become a hindrance to the church. So many young Christians are hiding in caves of bitterness and frustration because some older saint felt threatened by the gift of the younger Christian and either said something or did something that caused the person to flee, never realizing their full potential in God. I have heard it said over and over again that no one is a success unless he has a successor. If you feel words you have spoken or things you have done caused someone to flee to a cave, go find him, apologize, encourage him in the Lord, impart wisdom, and become active in helping him reach his full potential in God. Share with them how God brought you, taught you, carried you and led you. Be an example of how God can use any body and when they ask how you can be so sure, you can say, He used me.

Shift change

For so long people have seen the church fights, the preacher/pastor sex scandals, money laundering, and church members who call themselves brothers and sisters tear one another apart with their tongues. Having grown up in this atmosphere myself, I often found myself asking the question "is this really the church?" We must stop the fighting and let the Holy Spirit govern the church.

People are beginning to understand the importance of loyalty to those considered brothers and sisters. They understand that in order to befriend someone you must first earn their trust by respecting them and their ideas. Too many church members have the mindset of it's their way or the highway. That wouldn't be so bad if the ones who were preaching this message were actually showing us how it looked by living it out in their daily lives. The time has come that the members of the church not only talk the talk, but walk the walk. We must allow this generation to tackle its problems the way God wants them to. They may have to go into clubs to bring their unsaved friends out. They may have to play different types of music to gain the ear of their unsaved friends. They may have to preach in other ways and in different forums other than church buildings to reach those who are lost. But whatever must be done, my God, if they have gained an understanding from God on how to get the job done, move over seasoned saints of God and pass the torch to the runners with the fresh legs and new ideas that they may win people to Jesus.

Don't be a hindrance to the church by taking root and refusing to move knowing you are ineffective. If your season has passed, accept it and let the next runner run. God expects you to put a whistle around your neck and coach the replacements. Wisdom tells us that there is a time to stay and there is a time to move out of the way. The church is not ours; it belongs to Jesus.

Chapter 2

The original game plan

For most of my life I have been involved in team sports. From football, to basketball, to track, to baseball, you name it. If it was a sport, I was ready to play. I remember playing games in the street as a young boy with all the guys and girls on my street. What fun we had! Although our games were not as organized as the professional games we watched on television, there was one thing that our little pick-up games had in common with the professionals, we had a game plan.

Even though we were young and were just playing for fun, it was evident the game would not be successful if everyone on the team did his own thing (We did allow the girls to play every now and then). If we wanted the game to be fun and really be a game, we needed to follow the rules of the game and have a specific game plan for our team. We didn't have a play- book, but we would gather in a circle and draw the next play on the ground. When everyone was given his/her assignment, we would break the huddle and run the designated play.

There was always one person responsible for drawing up the plays. You could call him the team leader. This person would usually be the one who either had the most experience playing the game or was the oldest on the team and none of the other players dared to question his authority. But one thing was for certain, if we were to be a part of the team, we had to follow the game plan of the team leader.

When Jesus said he would build his church, he did not speak those words without having the game plan or the mission of the church in mind. On a mountain in Galilee, Jesus assembled his team and gave them the game plan.

"All authority in heaven and on earth has been given to me.
Therefore go and make disciples of all nations, baptizing

them in the name of the Father, and of the Son and of the Holy Spirit, and teaching them to obey everything I have commanded you. And surely I am with you always, to the very end of the age" (Matthew 28:18-20 NIV).

The game plan was fourfold:
- go
- make disciples
- baptize
- teach them to obey everything I have commanded you

This was the mission. This was the game plan. Not only did he give them what to do, but he also left them with the assurance that they could accomplish the mission because he would always be with them *to the very end of the age.* They would never be alone. No matter how hard it got on the road to fulfilling the mission, He would be right by their side. Take a look at the church today. Is the original mission still our mission today or have we diverted to our own missions? The mission is repeated again in Acts 2:8.

You will be My witnesses in Jerusalem, and in all Judea and Samaria, and to the ends of the earth."

Behind every mission there is a motive and a desired end. When we speak of motive, we ask the question, why? Why am I doing what I am doing? Am I doing what I am doing to be seen of men or am I doing what I am doing to glorify the name of Jesus? Am I doing what I am doing for financial gain or am I doing what I am doing as investment into the kingdom of God? We discussed the issue of jealousy earlier but another problem that is destroying the church is the issue of distorted motives- doing what you do for the wrong reasons. Jesus exposed the motives of certain religious leaders as they gave to the needy, prayed and fasted.

"Beware of practicing your righteousness before men to be noticed by them; otherwise you have no reward with your Father who is in heaven When therefore you give alms, do not sound a trumpet before you, as the hypocrites do in the synagogues and in the streets, that they may be honored

by men. Truly I say to you, they have their reward in full."
(Matthew 6:1-2)

Jesus warned us to be careful not to do our acts of righteousness before men, to be seen by them because if we do, we will have no reward from our Father in heaven. God searches the hearts of men for the motivation behind what they do. How many songs are being sung, sermons being preached, welcomes being extended, money being given, all under the disguise that "I love the Lord," when in reality, the Lord is no where on our mind? It's time that the church realizes that God will not give us power for our own plans. We have our own hidden agendas as we give leadership in certain areas of the church and then we wonder why things don't turn out the way we planned. Paul told the church at Corinth that the Lord would come and bring to light the things hidden in the darkness and disclose the motives of men's hearts; and then each man's praise will come to him from God (1 Corinthians 4:5). When the light is turned on, will your Father in Heaven have a reason to praise you?

The atmosphere in the church today is thick with pleasing man rather than pleasing God. We are acting as if man has a heaven or hell to put us in. According to the word of God, there was only one man who came and died for the sins of the world, and it's Him alone that I long to please. Man can do a lot of things for me, but none of these things will last for eternity. Only what we do for Jesus Christ will last.

Our rewards in heaven will be based on what we did for Christ on earth.

> *For no man can lay a foundation other than the one which is laid, which is Jesus Christ. Now if any man builds upon the foundation with gold, silver, precious stones, wood, hay, straw, each man's work will become evident; for the day will show it, because it is to be revealed with fire; and the fire itself will test the quality of each man's work. If any man's work which he has built upon it remains, he shall receive a reward. If any man's work is burned up, he shall suffer loss; but he himself shall be saved, yet so as through fire (1 Corinthians 3: 11-15).*

It doesn't mater how much money you have given or how long you have served in the church. If what you've done was not done with the right motive, when everyone else is in line in heaven receiving rewards for the things they have done and you are left empty handed, you will have no one to blame but yourself. If what you have done up to this point in life has all been done to win the approval of men or to have someone call your name, repent and ask God to change your heart. We will deal with this issue of the heart in a later chapter, but God is searching for men and women whose hearts are pure towards him and his mission. It's not about us. It's all about Him. Once we come to this realization, we won't worry the slightest about who will receive the credit or who will the people like the best, the only thing that will matter is that we played a part in fulfilling the mission.

However, we need to be reminded that if we continue to serve God with distorted motives, we may make it to heaven, but we will walk through the pearly gates smelling like smoke.

Fueled by God's power

Recently my wife and I purchased a new car. It was the car my wife had dreamed of owning. This car is considered one of the top of the line vehicles on the market today. With its black leather interior and its sleek silver exterior, we were driving in style.

However, we would soon learn a valuable lesson. Although this top of the line vehicle was a nice vehicle, there was something this car needed that without it made this vehicle nothing more than a show toy.

One day we were on our way to a little league football meeting, just the two of us when the vehicle began to make these sudden stops. As the vehicle continued to make these annoying motions, I noticed the low fuel light had come on. Now I had not read the owners manual, but I knew that before this car would run out of gas, it would give me some other signal that the gas was just about gone. As we continued to drive and I passed one gas station after another, I knew we would make it to the meeting without having to stop. Guess what, we didn't! This top of the line vehicle stopped in the middle of the street without notifying me further that we were running out of gas. As I tried to push the car and my wife steered, I soon realized that the car had done its part; it displayed the low fuel light to inform me that it was time to re-fuel. That light indicated that we needed to pull over right away and get some gas. But because I felt we could make it, I disregarded the warning sign and continued on.

How many in the church has God given the warning sign that your gas tank is low? You are trying to operate on the fumes of your own strength and power and God is telling you that this machine, the church, will only run on his power. Your education, your popularity, your eloquence of speech, neither your melodious voice can power this machine. If the church is going to run, it must run on God's fuel and God's power. God's program will be fueled by God's power. He is not obligated to fuel anything we plan outside of what He wants to do. One reason the church today is experiencing so many failures is that we are asking God to give us power to do the things we want to do and have placed the things He wants done on the back burner. We want our membership size to increase, not because we are concerned about souls, but because we are in competition with the guy down the street. If you are trying to accomplish something using God's name for your purposes, you will be out there on your own pushing your machine on an empty tank of gas. Believe me, it's no fun!

Our strength is not sufficient to accomplish great things in the kingdom of God. We can no longer allow just anyone to preach in the pulpit. We can no longer allow just anyone to sing in the choir. We can no longer ordain deacons because they are long time friends and appoint people to boards because their pockets run deep. The business of the church is not "you scratch my back and I'll scratch yours", the business of the church is to make disciples of men. When we decide to get back to the business of the church; helping those who are less fortunate, seeking to please God and not man, being an example to the world and not conforming to the ways of the world, we will experience God's power like we have never experienced it before.

So go and make disciples! Baptize them and teach them to obey all that Jesus Christ has taught you through your obedience to Him.

Where Do We Go From Here?

The remaining chapters of the book will focus on the qualities the first century church displayed at its inception in Acts 2 and beyond. The picture painted for us in the pages of Acts show us what the church should be and the results of being this kind of church.

Much of what the early church experienced was a direct result of being led and empowered by the Holy Spirit. They didn't have all the wonderful programs we have today, but they had power. They didn't have all of the boards we have today, but they were unified. They didn't have all the bible knowledge we have today, but they preached the gospel of the kingdom and men were saved.

In no way am I trying to convey that the church of today is either useless or very far off from the first church. On the contrary, the church is doing many wonderful things in the name of Jesus Christ our Lord. Whatever we do, it must be done first and foremost to bring glory to our Lord. When we talk about salvation in the church today, Jesus as Savior is evident in the lives of our members. We sing and praise God for sending Jesus to die on the cross for our sins. We have made salvation a personal thing, and although Jesus died for you and me, He died for you and me in the context of dying for the church.   As a member of the church, my salvation doesn't belong only to me, it belongs to the community God has saved me to. Throughout the pages of scripture, God has always blessed his people through covenant and community.

Not just for me

The story of Abraham sheds light on the New Testament idea of how God works through individuals to bless a people. Scripture doesn't identify for us the reason God chose Abraham, we simply read that he did and that's good enough for me. When you look back over your life before God saved you, if you would be honest you were not really looking for God. Many of the activities we were engaged in, we enjoyed. It's hard to convince a person to let something go that he enjoys. We often hear it said, "When I found Jesus." Well, the truth is we didn't find Him, he found us.

In the Old Testament, we read about Abraham, Isaac, Jacob, Joseph, Joshua, Nehemiah, Samuel, Ruth, Esther, David, and the list goes on and on. God called each of these individuals for a particular purpose but the purpose was not for self-gratification. God did some wonderful things through these people, but what he did through them was not for them. God's ultimate plan was to bless the covenant people of God and to bring them closer to Him. What God does for a person and through a person is not just for the person, it's for all of God's people to enjoy. Everything God does for the believer is for the benefit of the community of faith.

Every now and then my wife allows me to do the grocery shopping. When I go, I go with one thing in mind and that is to get what needs to be gotten and get out! If it's coffee, whatever coffee I see first that's the coffee I get. Whatever bread I see first, that's the bread I get. Whatever cheese I see first, I get it. Get the picture! When I leave the store, I feel a sense of relief and completion, however, when I get home and unpack the groceries, the stare of my wife lets me know that I have done something wrong. She begins to say things like, "this isn't real cheese." "Why did you get this off brand coffee?" "This bread won't stay fresh long." What she is saying to me in these cases is stop bringing home the imitation and bring home in the words of Coca-Cola , "the real thing."

The church in Acts 2 was the real thing. There was nothing to compare her to and whatever was done was by the leading of the Holy Spirit. There were no distorted motives and no sense of jealously among the people. The Holy Spirit was the orchestrator of events and pleasing Jesus Christ by fulfilling his mission was the goal.

If we want to see the awesome power of God working through the church we must investigate why the early church was so successful and incorporate that philosophy into what we are doing today.

Chapter 3

Life-Changing Messages

Now when they heard this, they were pierced to the heart, and said to Peter and the rest of the apostles, Brethren, what shall we do? (Acts 2:37)

The heart is a very sensitive part of human nature. Hearts can be broken. Hearts can be discouraged. Hearts can be manipulated. Often hearts can become so distraught that they give up on all that is right. The church has become too careless in simply telling fellow brothers and sisters in Christ to hang in there when times get hard. It's easy to tell a single parent not to give up on his or her child when you have a spouse to share the child-rearing responsibilities with. It's easy to tell someone to trust in God when you've never been through a storm that not even momma, daddy, pastor, cousin or friend could help you out of and you had to totally lean on God. People need to hear more than catchy clichés and powerless prayers, they need to hear and see life changing messages by true believers of the Lord Jesus Christ. It's through these life messages, orchestrated by the Holy Spirit, that people's hearts are stirred to ask the question, "What must I do?" When people begin to ask this question, then and only then can the process of mending broken hearts and lives begin.

Every day people find themselves in situations where their faith is being put on trial, and because they are not firmly rooted in Jesus Christ, the enemy attacks their mind and heart to the point where they are easily manipulated by evil spirits. The fact that we live in a world where everyone has not accepted Jesus Christ as their Lord and Savior and others who believe their happiness is all that matters even to the expense of causing pain to others, we are prime candidates for broken hearts. Even the strongest of Christians have experienced broken hearts. When you've helped people and those same people turn around and mistreat you that can cause a broken heart. When those who you long to receive affirmation from take part in scandalizing your name, that can cause a broken heart. I'm not talking about people at your job. I'm talking about your brothers and sisters in Christ. I'm talking about people who call you for advice when their marriage is on the skid. I'm talking about people who ask you to talk to their children because they don't know what else to do.

I thank God for the family I was raised in. If any one were to ask me what mistakes my parents made in raising three sons, I would have to say none. And even if they did, I can't recognize them even to this day. I say that to say this: None of us are where we are because of our own doing. It took the love and care of many people who God strategically placed in our lives to mold us into vessels worthy to be used by Him. Thank God for the morals you were taught. Thank God for the lessons you learned early in life. Thank God for setting you apart from the norm and making you comfortable in being what He created you to be. I say all of this to make this crucial point-Don't allow others to make you feel bad about your godly lifestyle and your walk with God. There is a spirit at work in the church that seeks to dilute the pursuit of godly lifestyles. Instead of glorifying God for being able to change us and keep us, we criticize those who have made God and His agenda priority in their lives.

Once I was talking to a young lady who for a good deal of time had been coming to me for advice. Now mind you, I did not volunteer or seek her out, she sought me out. As long as I was helping her, I was thanked for being a godly man, a man of integrity. She often commented on the love she saw between my wife and I and our children. In her eyes, I was a pretty neat guy. But once when she did not do something that she was supposed to do, I asked her about it and from that, I witnessed something that grew me up in 30 minutes. This young lady who I had talked to and prayed for, turned on me as if I were the enemy. She told me that I got on her nerves with my self-righteous self. Now I had heard this statement made about my family from a few other people, all of whom were individuals who felt they could do what they wanted at all times answering to no one. Well my personality dictates that all things should be done decently and in order. We all have to be accountable to someone as we live in the world; without accountability, there would be complete chaos. If we are able to submit to worldly authority, people like police officers, supervisors and government officials; we should submit more to spiritual authority for these are the people who watch over our souls. When we submit to worldly authority and rebel against spiritual authority, we find ourselves as a nation and church in the position of Israel recorded in the book of Judges.

> *In those days there was no king in Israel; every man did what was right in his own eyes (Judges 17:6).*

Today as in the day of Micah the prophet, people are placing their own interest before the desperate needs of others and even before those things that are right. People today are rejecting God's way of living and as a result our world is suffering. Anyone who does not submit to God's way of doing things will end up doing whatever seems right to them at the time. Christians must realize and accept that this tendency is present within us as well. If we neglect to get closer to God and stay close, we will find ourselves drifting and relying more on our desire of acquiring things than on the ways and heart of God. We must begin to live like what is in God's heart is much more important to us than what is in His hands. It is evident that the church views God as a cosmic Santa Claus whose only job is to drop off things to us that we have prayed for. Our prayers are filled with asking for what we want from God with very little asking of God what He wants from us! I believe God is sitting on His throne just waiting for us to ask Him, "God, what can I do for you today?" Listen to what the bible says about those whose hearts belong to God.

> *For the eyes of the Lord move to and fro throughout the earth that He may strongly support those whose heart is completely His (2 Chronicles 16:9).*

What an awesome statement! To know that God is looking for people that He can strongly support. The fact that God has to look for anything simply blows my mind! Not only that, but to know that God is willing and waiting to support us not just a little, but strongly (I like that word strongly), if we give our hearts completely to Him. When we live to please Him and daily seek His heart, He in turn will take care of us and support us in such a way we could never take care of ourselves. If there were ever a promise for us to claim in these times, it is that God will strongly support those whose hearts completely belong to Him. Listen to what God told a young man who was truly in need of His support.

> *Now it came about after the death of Moses the servant of the Lord that the Lord spoke to Joshua the son of Nun, Moses' servant, saying, "Moses my servant is dead; now therefore arise, cross this Jordan, you and all this people, to the land which I am giving to them, to the sons of Israel. Every place on which the sole of your foot treads, I have given to you, just as I spoke to Moses (Joshua 1:1-3).*

Here is a young man who has just had the responsibility of leading a nation placed on his shoulders. The task was great, the people were many, and there were battles to be fought, not to mention the shoes of Moses he was now to fill. What a task! What pressure! But here is a young man whose heart belonged completely to God. He had faith in God and believed that if God had His back just as He had Moses', he would be successful. But wait a minute, look what else God says to this young man whose heart belonged completely to Him.

> *No man will be able to stand before you all the days of your life. Just as I have been with Moses, I will be with you; I will not fail you or forsake you. Be strong and courageous, for you shall give this people possession of the land which I swore to their fathers to give them. Only be strong and very courageous; be careful to do according to all the law which Moses My servant commanded you; do not turn from it to the right or to the left, so that you may have success wherever you go (Joshua 1:5-7).*

The support and success that God promises can be claimed by individuals whose hearts are completely His. Just as God's support of Joshua was based on Joshua's heart toward Him and his willingness to obey (don't turn to the right are left), so must we give our hearts completely to Him to receive His strong support and the promise of being successful in all we do.

Spiritual Leadership

Where there is no spiritual leadership, people will do whatever they want to do. Where there is no standard, people have nothing to shoot for. If we allow people to make us feel bad about our godly lifestyle so they can feel good about their sinful lifestyle, we set ourselves up for conformity. All of us at one point have asked, "Is it worth all of this?" When I was hanging out with my old friends I was happier, had more money in my pocket, and I could do whatever I wanted to do. If the enemy can cause those of us who are striving to live holy to cover our lips and not speak up for what is right or even turn around, our life message is no longer bringing glory to God but elevating Satan because it seems that Satan has turned one of God's children around. Godly lifestyles have the power to turn even the hardest heart to God and the enemy knows this. If he can get us to conform to the world's systems, then we lose our witness and we are just like everyone else. Paul gives us a clear directive concerning this issue because he was aware of the negative effects conformity would have on the spreading of the gospel if the people of God yielded to the influences of the world.

> *I urge you therefore, brethren, by the mercies of God, to present your bodies a living and holy sacrifice, acceptable to God, which is your spiritual service of worship (Romans 12:1).*

Throughout the Old Testament, animal sacrifice was important in the life of God's chosen people. However, we must never forget that although sacrifice was important, it is clear that obedience from the heart was God's ultimate desire and was valued higher than sacrifice. We must be careful that our sacrifices to God are not without obedience to God. God wants us to offer ourselves, not animals, as living sacrifices as we offer our all to Him to use as He sees fit. The animals were offered from a grateful heart that their sins had been forgiven. When we offer our bodies to God as living sacrifices and live in obedience to Him, we do so as well from a grateful heart that our sins have been forgiven. If people in your church are doing whatever they want, check the lifestyles of the leadership and the standard being set.

Where there is no vision, the people are unrestrained, But happy is he who keeps the law (Proverbs 29:18).

We must begin to cast vision for lifestyle. Vision is cast to build buildings and to establish businesses, but how often is vision cast to develop godly lifestyles? If there is no vision cast for godly living, then all we can expect is for people to conform to the lifestyle of the world. We have to give people a picture of what godly living looks like and the benefits it brings. Not to say everything will be fine all the time, but living for Jesus is the most fulfilling life a person can live. When we present our bodies to God as living and holy sacrifices, we will not be conformed to this world, but be transformed by the renewing of our mind, that we may prove what the will of God is, that which is good and acceptable and perfect (Romans 12:2, paraphrased).

The walk and relationship we have with God is more important than money and buildings. It's good to have buildings and money but when people who are claiming to be Christians have little or no desire to live holy, we have a problem. Our goal is to get to heaven and to take as many people with us as we can. Erecting buildings won't do it. Amassing enormous budgets won't do it. We must live what we preach and sing about. It has been said the greatest deterrent from the church is its people. If we don't live godly lives, we are ineffective and a hindrance to the mission. Let me get back to my story.

As I sat there listening to this lady's vicious attack, I realized some of the things that were coming out of her mouth were not her own, they were things she had heard others say about me. When I asked her to tell me what self-righteous meant, all she could say was, "I don't know but that's what you are." She added, "I don't want to be anything like you. I don't want people to think I am holy. I want people to accept me smoking a little, drinking a little. I want them to accept me." Well to make a long story short, her intent was to make me feel guilty about my lifestyle. Her goal was to try to get me to agree with her that it was alright to use drugs, alright to practice homosexuality, alright to lie, steal and cheat. As I looked at her, I could see the bitterness and unhappiness that her lifestyle was affording her, but yet she was criticizing a life that was full of joy and peace. When we listen to Satan tell us that we can enjoy the Christian life and live in the world at the same time, we have been tricked. She wanted me to affirm her belief that it is alright for people to give their best in worldly endeavors but when it comes to the things of God, we can give Him our leftovers. Well I was not going to give her that pleasure. I believe God does not want our leftovers, He wants our best! So the conflict arises between those who seek to serve God with all their strength and might and those who have made Jesus their Savior but not their Lord. As you read these words and you are one of the people who is always serving, always faithful, always trying to do what's right but are always criticized and you feel all alone, let me encourage you, you are not alone. Those who experience these types of attacks are those who Jesus gave the title of "salt." Without salt in the world and in the church, all hope disappears. If you are feeling now as I once felt, "What's the use?" "Is it all worth it?" "Maybe I should lower my standards." "Maybe I should stop reading my bible daily." Well let me tell you don't fall into the trap. You are what you are for God's glory. Those same people who are trying to tear you apart and break your heart are only tools that are making you stronger. Don't get angry with them, continue to pray for them knowing that "all things work out for the good of them who love God and are called according to His purpose" (Romans 8:28). His purpose is to glorify Himself in the world and He does that through the lives of faithful men, women, boys and girls. Here are a few suggestions on how to handle these attacks:

1. **Pray against retaliation because when we hold our peace and allow the Lord to fight our battles, the result is God is glorified and men are edified.**
2. **Fast for victory over the spirit of weariness. Claim that you will "reap a harvest if you don't give up."**

3. **Never allow someone to belittle your relationship with the Lord. Only you know what God brought you through to get you where you are today.**
4. **Don't stop praising Him.**
5. **Don't stop serving Him.**
6. **Don't stop being faithful because your labor is not in vain.**

The tenacity to stick it out when you feel like quitting is a life changing message to someone who is on the verge of giving up. What we need today are more people who will stick it out in the trenches of life and will not compromise their faith at any cost. Will you be one of the few, the proud, God's faithful servant? Don't conform. Don't allow others to get you off track but strive to get them on the right track! You are important to God and when you live a life that pleases Him, you lift up Jesus and through you others will see Him. They will see His love, His forgiveness, and His longsuffering. They will see the joy He brings and the peace He gives. When we lift Him up, He promises that "I will draw all men unto me." (John 12:32)

If you desire to be a living message of the goodness of God, pray and ask God to send people in your life with the same passion you have to be faithful and hold up the banner where you have been planted. Allow your life to become a message to others that says there is a blessing in serving the true and living God. Keep on loving Him. Keep on obeying Him. When you feel like you are all alone because of your stand for Jesus Christ and righteousness, remember God's eye is upon you and He is strongly supporting you and the outcome will be success.

Guard Your Heart

When the word heart is mentioned, we often think of the muscular organ that receives blood from the veins and pumps it through the arteries to oxygenate the blood. It is a confusing statement for a child or new believers when we say, "love God with all your heart." Can we love God with a muscular organ? This is not the idea expressed in phrases such as: "My heart goes out to you." "His heart was in the right place." "This is from the bottom of my heart." "We need to have a heart to heart talk." Take a look at the following scriptures referencing the heart.

> *My son, do not forget my teaching, but let your heart keep my commandments (Proverbs 3:1).*

> *Trust the Lord with all your heart and do not lean on your own understanding (Proverbs 3:5).*

> *Watch over your heart with all diligence, for from it flow the springs of life (Proverbs 4:23).*

> *For out of the heart come evil thoughts, murders, adulteries, fornications, thefts, false witness, slanders (Matthew 15:19)*

> *... for God sees not as man sees, for man looks at the outward appearance, but the Lord looks at the heart (1 Samuel 16:7).*

> *Let the words of my mouth and the meditation of my heart be acceptable in thy sight, O Lord, my rock and my Redeemer (Psalm 19:14).*

When the bible talks about the heart, it defines it as our deepest, innermost feelings. In the bible, the spectrum of human emotions is attributed to the heart. In short, we can define the biblical usage of the word heart as the seat of our emotions. It is here that decisions are made. It is here that personalities are forged. It is here that perceptions are formed. Society is what it is today not because of the President, not because of the ozone layer, not because of unemployment and not because of racism; all that has happened and is happening stems from the heart condition of men, women, boys and girls. The killing, stealing, abortion, divorce, suicide, and drug abuse are all issues of life that are manifestations of corrupt and polluted hearts. This is why the writer of Proverbs 4:23 commands us to "watch over our hearts."

When we become fearful, the word of God gives us a word of encouragement through one of His most faithful servants, the Apostle Paul.

> *"For God has not given us the spirit of timidity, but of power and love and discipline. Therefore do not be ashamed of the testimony of our Lord, or of me His prisoner; but join with me in suffering for the gospel according to the power of God, who has saved us, and called us with a holy calling, not according to our works, but according to His own purpose and grace which was granted us in Christ Jesus from all eternity (2 Timothy 1:7-9).*

When fear tries to control your heart, you are aware that it is a tactic of the enemy to try to infiltrate your heart and take control. Speak the Word of God into whatever you are dealing with at that time and send the devil on the run. We must be on guard not to allow anything and everything to slip into our hearts. You have the power within you to guard your heart. Use it.

Our worldview and life view are determined by the music we listen to, the company we keep, the books we read, the shows we watch, the language we use and most importantly what we do with Jesus Christ. To guard our hearts, we must make obeying the word of God priority number one in our lives. When we compromise it, we create an open door for the enemy to slip in and do damage to our hearts.

Matters of the heart

Each of us has been ministered to by someone and the words they spoke to us either encouraged us to make drastic changes in our lives or persuaded us to go in the wrong direction. We were either given the truth with no holds barred, we may have been given the truth with a lot of sugar on it, or maybe we were even given a flat out lie. Regardless of what we were given, in our heart we had to make a decision about what we were going to do with what had been given to us.

If we are not careful, the enemy will take what's in our heart and use it against us. The apostles could have used the fact that the same people who they had been commissioned to share the gospel with had been the same people who killed Jesus and refused to share the message with them, but that was not the case. They did not allow what others had said and done affect their responsibility to share the gospel. Often our incorrect perception of people and their deeds trigger a sense of negativity in us. We cannot make decisions about people unless we have walked in their shoes and have a clear understanding of why they behave the way they do. When people engage in activities that are morally and spiritually incorrect, we have a tendency to respond to them negatively or not at all. We would like to see them change and often our heart goes out to them, but often instead of loving them and trying to lead them to Christ, we become frustrated. Frustration can be a dangerous emotional condition in a Christian's life.

The spirit of frustration is at work in the body of Christ. It is found between individuals, church groups, and church denominations. In a world of different points of view, different motives whether right or wrong, there is constant unrest in the hearts and minds of believers. But listen, before God can use the church like He wants, we first must be usable. If we cannot get along with one another, how can we be light to others? I believe the enemy has manipulated a powerful weapon of change that God has given us. As believers we must agree with God that we are the salt of the earth. If we lose our saltiness, the bible says we are good for nothing. We lose our saltiness when we become frustrated with one another and with others. We lose our saltiness when we preach and sing one message and live another. When salt is added to anything, it changes the flavor of whatever it was added to. Because of what it is, it does what it does: It changes what it touches. Because of who we are, we have the power to change what we come in contact with. Our object of change is not a piece of meat, our object of change is the world, and God has placed within us a motivational weapon that causes us to be who we are and to do what we do. That weapon is found in all of us and many of us are unaware of it. It is called a burden.

God Uses Our Burdens

So the king said to me, "Why is your face sad though you are not sick? This is nothing but sadness of heart" (Nehemiah 2:2).

The book of Nehemiah opens with Nehemiah receiving word of the horrible conditions of his people in Jerusalem. Their cities have been destroyed. They are ridiculed by their neighbors and the gates and walls that served as their protection have been destroyed. The news floors Nehemiah. His heart is crushed. Sleepless nights ensue. His mind constantly dwells on the condition of his homeland. He feels he must do something, but what?

Knowledge of the condition of his homeland burdened Nehemiah so that the king recognized his distress. Some things should bother us so that others ought to be able to tell. People who have no concern about anything other than themselves have a heart problem. They have no compassion.

In our hustle and bustle world, we seldom see the deplorable conditions others are living in. The world needs more good Samaritans and fewer religious show-offs.

Think about this for a moment. Every day we drive a particular way to work, school, or wherever our destination may be. Along our route there are businesses, billboards, and various other objects along the road. Try right now to list on a sheet of paper ten billboards and their content. I guarantee you will be hard pressed to accomplish this task. Why? In our haste to get to where we are going and to do what is on our agenda, we subconsciously tune out our surroundings. We rarely take time to notice things that do not directly affect us.

Everyone seems to be able to identify problems. "What they need to do over at that church is ...!" "If I was in that position I would ...!" "Our schools are in really bad shape!" The world doesn't need another problem identifier. What the world needs are people who see problems and get involved to bring about change. The words of Jesus speak clearly to this mindset of problem identification only.

And He was saying to them, "The harvest is plentiful, but the laborers are few; therefore beseech the Lord of the harvest to send out laborers into His harvest (Luke 10:2).

We are not special because we can recognize problems. God wants us to seek His face for solutions because He already knows the problems. If we don't have a burden concerning that particular problem, we will not see the need to seek direction and get involved. Jesus tells us that there is much work to do. There are problems everywhere. The issue is not whether we can recognize the problems; however, it is that those who recognize the problems do nothing beyond that. We must pray that God would quicken the hearts of believers everywhere to see ourselves as agents of change. We must disperse into the fields of this world as laborers with God-given burdens, armed with the power of the Holy Spirit, and equipped with revelation from God as how to handle and solve the problems in our homes, churches, communities, and the world.

If you are a child of God, there should be some things that bother you to the point where you just have to get involved. When I see parents neglect their children, it bothers me and I have to get involved. When I see husbands neglect their wives and wives neglect their husbands, it bothers me and I get involved. When I see churches invest the majority of their resources into adults and issue a few crumbs to its children, that bothers me and I get involved.

However, there was a period in my life when I said to heck with it all. I had become so frustrated with the ignorance of some people that I wanted to pack up, move, and start all over again with different people. Things I once enjoyed doing like going to church, hanging out with people, became unbearable. I was to the point that I saw the problems, but the frustration I felt toward the people left no room for compassion in my heart to try to help them and lead them to the right path. It took several sleepless nights before I clearly understood what God was saying to me in that period of frustration. I had become angry with people who claimed to be Christians but behaved contrarily. The Holy Spirit spoke to me as I was on my way home one Wednesday afternoon and said this: the enemy has turned the burdens I have placed on your heart into areas of frustration in your life. Instead of you dealing with the burdens with love and understanding you are fleeing from them in anger and frustration. The reason you feel so strongly about these issues is because I want you to be a change agent where you are concerning these issues.

At once, my anger subsided. People who I had become frustrated with, my heart went out to them and God gave me strategies of how to deal with them. God revealed to me that in my frustration and anger, I was not doing anything positive to affect the situations. I constantly found myself being critical of people instead of ministering to them. I found myself avoiding those who really needed my help. God revealed that when He gives us burdens He also equips us with what we need to bring about a change in the area we are burdened. No where else is this demonstrated more clearly than in the book of Nehemiah. Nehemiah chapter two lists several things God provides to help us deal with our burdens.

- ### *God provides realization that it must be done His way.*

Then the king said to me, "What would you request?" So I prayed to the God of heaven (Nehemiah 2:4).

How often has God placed a burden on your heart and you decided to do something about it and developed a plan of attack before consulting Him? Before Nehemiah did anything, he consulted God. Nehemiah prayed for direction. We must be careful to remember that our way of dealing with issues may not be God's way. His thoughts are higher than our thoughts and His ways are higher than our ways. If a change is to occur in the lives, actions, and attitudes of others through us, we must follow God's plan of achieving His objectives and He will reveal His plan through prayer and His Word.

- ### *God provides authority and favor*

And the king granted them to me because the good hand of my God was on me (Nehemiah 2:8b).

The fact that God placed that particular burden on you is proof that He has given you power and authority to go wherever you must go. Opposition will arise; however, when it sees that you come with authority, opposition has to move aside and sometimes those who meant to do you harm, God causes them to help you in your cause. What a mighty God we serve!

Nehemiah found favor in the sight of the king and the king was willing to assist Nehemiah in his mission. We will look at favor at work in the life of Joseph in a later chapter but we must understand that when God's good hand is on a person, nothing can stop him. Nehemiah tells us that the good hand of God was on him. So no matter the condition of the city that he sought to rebuild, it had to change for the better for the simple fact that he had a burden and God's good hand of favor was on him to be the agent of change. When the good hand of God is on you, no matter how bad things may seem, walls may be down, gates burned down, marriage on the brink, finances at an all time low, no joy or hope in sight, when you come into the picture, things change. Why? It's not because of you, but it is because He placed that burden on you so He could work through you to be an agent of change. However, there is one thing we must remember; we must be careful not to use the favor of God for our own twisted motives.

- *God provides proper equipment and supplies to get the job done.*

"If it please the king, let letters be given me for the governors of the provinces beyond the River, that they may allow me to pass through until I come to Judah, and a letter to Asaph the keeper of the king's forest, that he may give me timber to make beams for the gates of the fortress which is by the temple, for the wall of the city, and for the house to which I will go." And the king granted them to me because the good hand of my God was on me (Nehemiah 2:8).

If God sends you on a mission for Him, He will supply all of your needs.

- *God provides protection for you.*

Then I came to the governors of the provinces beyond the River and gave them the king's letters. Now the king had sent with me officers of the army and horsemen (Nehemiah 2:9).

Nehemiah could go about accomplishing his mission because the king had appointed his officers to accompany Nehemiah and protect him. Whenever we are in route to rebuild what the devil has torn down, the enemy will try to kill us. But just as Nehemiah was protected by the king's officers, we are protected by God's officers; His mighty angels. Wherever we go, God's angels are around us, escorting us from destination to destination and protecting us from dangers seen and unseen.

Don't allow the enemy to change your God- given burden into an area of frustration in your life. The only way Satan can have his way in the world is for God's children to turn their back on the world. If God's people stop caring and give up, all hope is lost for those outside of Christ. Allow that burden to move you to action. Speak when God tells you to speak. Move when God tells you to move. Build when He tells you to build knowing that He has given you the plan, the favor, the resources, and the protection to accomplish what He has called you to do.

What to Say

The events in Acts chapter 2 are crucial to church life today and were sparked by a life-changing word spoken by the apostle Peter. The first sermon of the church is recorded in verses 14-36 and through these stirring words of truth people of all walks of life were forced to make a decision whether to accept and follow Jesus or reject Him. No middle ground was offered. No other way was addressed because there was and is no other way. The way is Jesus. That's all, nothing else. If you need peace, get Jesus. If you need joy, get Jesus. If you're looking for stability, get Jesus. The truth is that without Jesus, you are nothing.

Peter preached the truth about Jesus. He was not preaching what he'd heard. He was preaching what he knew. This same man who had denied Jesus now had power to lead others to Jesus. How? It was in the message. Jesus said the truth we know will set us free. Was Jesus simply saying it's enough to simply know intellectually the truth and that will set you free? I don't think so. Simply knowing what the truth is will not change a person. Most of us know that lying is wrong, but we still do it. We know that stealing is wrong, but we still do it. Simply knowing what's right is not enough. When you know what the truth is and obey it, it's that truth that sets you free. Peter's message was laced with truth, conviction, and compassion. The effectiveness of the message is demonstrated in the response of the listeners in their question, "Brethren what shall we do?" When we allow God to fill us with his Holy Spirit, what we preach and teach will have the power to pierce men's hearts that they will want to yield their lives to Jesus Christ.

The critical elements found in Peter's message were:
- Jesus was and is a real person (2:22)
- Jesus was crucified and resurrected (23-24)
- Everything that happened had already been prophesied (25-35)
- Jesus is the Messiah (2:36)
- Everyone who repents and turns to Jesus Christ in faith will be forgiven and given the gift of the Holy Spirit (37-38).

Centering our teaching and preaching on these elements brings hope to the life of the hearer. All that was foretold happened and this gives us hope and confidence that we can trust what the bible says.

How lives are changed

Everyone wants to live a productive life. No one grows up saying I want to be a drug addict or a homeless person. So how have so many people's lives turned out opposite to what they wanted? The key to unlocking this mystery is in the word want. They wanted, and that's all. Everyone wants something. The six-year-old boy wants a bicycle for his birthday. The twelve-year-old girl wants to wear lipstick and fingernail polish. The adult male wants a nice home for his family and the adult female wants her children to do great in school. Everyone wants something; however, what we want often does not show up in our actions and decisions. We see what we want, but what it takes to receive it never crosses our minds and seldom do we take the time to count the cost.

Suppose one of you wants to build a tower. Will he first not sit down and estimate the cost to see if he has enough money to complete it? For if he lays the foundation and is not able to finish it, everyone who sees it will ridicule him, saying, 'This fellow began to build and was not able to finish" (Luke 14:28-30, NIV).

"We can do all things through Jesus Christ who gives us strength." Philippians 4:13 is one of the most familiar passages of scripture known. We quote it in sermons and short talks. We even post it on signs. In all of our use of this passage, I believe too many of us miss out on the fact that Paul says, "I can do." As long as we continue to want but never do, our situations will never change. One definition of insanity is to do the same thing over and over again and expect a different result. Well, so many Christians have wanted revival to sweep over their church and city, but never fast and pray for it to happen. Parents have wanted their children to behave in school and respect authority, but never discipline their children or teach them how to respect authority by setting the example themselves. Pastors and preachers have wanted their members and listeners to obey God's word, but either their preaching is irrelevant or they don't live what they preach. Any baker will tell you it's not enough to just want a cake, you must get in the kitchen, mix the ingredients, sweat over a hot oven, and after you have followed the instructions and a little time has passed, you are able to enjoy the fruit, or should I say "cake" of your labor.

So I say to you as you take this message to heart. Change is just one step away in your life. Say good-bye right now to being just a person who only wants, and say hello to the new you. Say hello to the new you who will be a doer and know that by making this decision, you have the power of the kingdom of heaven behind you because the enabling power of God's precious Holy Spirit will guide you and empower you to accomplish what you want by granting you strength in your doing.

You can do it

It's safe to say most people enjoy sporting events. Watching the players compete to defeat their opponent. We marvel at the strength of the players and their resilience to persevere, however, if we are not careful, we overlook one of the most important people of all. This person is usually on the sidelines, pacing back and forth, carefully calculating the strategy of the team and its next move. Any idea who this person is? You guessed it, the coach. The strategist. The overseer. The motivator.

As spectators, what we see on game day from the coach is not what the players see during the week. During practice, the coach is constantly riding the backs of his players in an effort to get the most out of them. Sometimes he is cool, at other times he is loud and wild. Whatever the case may be, the coach's ultimate goal is to inspire his players to be the best they can be. If the opposing team will be a difficult challenge, he lets them know. If playing conditions are horrible, he lets them know. Whatever the players need to know in order to compete, the coach lays it all out in the game plan.

All of us need a coach in our Christian lives. Someone who will tell us what we need to hear. Not only will that person tell us the truth and expect the best from us, but will discipline us when we do not obey the instructions laid forth.

A slave will not be instructed by words alone; For though he understands, there will be no response (Proverbs 29:19).

This wise saying speaks to what the church is facing today. People have become content with simply hearing the word. We have more bible teaching in this period of human history than in any other time. We have more books, tapes, CD's, and other valuable sources of information all at our fingertips. Whatever we want to know, we can find the answer to our question. But just knowing is not enough. James, the brother of Jesus put it best when he said the gospel is a message to obey, not just to listen to. If you don't obey, you are only fooling yourself (James 1:22, LASB). The time has come for those who know the truth and are living the truth to stand up for righteousness when others are content with only hearing and not obeying. We must stop giggling in the presence of sin. Stop implying that we approve by not speaking up. When a good coach sees something wrong, he blows his whistle, the action stops, and he corrects the problem. The same way a good coach deals with negligence and disobedience, we as God's ambassadors in the world must take our hands off our mouths, put a whistle in, and blow loudly, causing a break in the action of sin so we can coach from God's word on how He would have us to live.

When I talk about blowing your whistle, we must be clear to understand before we can blow our whistles in the world, we must first blow them in the church. It doesn't make sense to blow our whistles in the world, have the world come to the church and see the very thing they left operating in the church. We must be accountable for our actions and lack of action. The Life Application Bible states Proverbs 29:19 in this way; "For a servant, mere words are not enough-discipline is needed. For the words may be understood, but they are not heeded."

Regardless of who you are, we all need someone to encourage us when we feel like giving up or turning around. We need people who will get in our face and tell us we can make it. Someone who will push us to be more than we think we can be and will tell us when we are right and when we are wrong. This person may not have a whistle around their neck, but the word of God in their heart coming out of their mouth will do just fine. If you know the word of God and are living it, become a coach in someone's life. Allow the truth God has revealed to you be a blessing in someone's life. The devil has his coaches out on the field, recruiting players with lies that if they follow his game plan they will enjoy money, power, and sex, unaware of the price of pain and regret they will someday reap. Someone needs the message God has given you. Someone needs to know the truth that hard work pays off and nothing in life is free except the gift of salvation that God gives to those who would accept His son Jesus Christ. Someone needs to know that if they obey God, they can be what He says they can be and they can have what He says they can have.

Don't just speak with your mouth, speak with your life. Everything you have gone through in life happened for a reason. Your life is a testimony of what God can do. Someone needs to know that God changes lives and you may be the person with the right message that propels that individual into their destiny.

Chapter 4

Devoted to the Kingdom

And they were continually devoting themselves...... (Acts 2:42).

You can tell what a person is devoted to by observing what they do the most. Find out what a person consistently does and you will know where that person's passion and devotion is. It disturbs me when Christians complain about the length of the worship service whether it is one hour, two hours, or even three hours, but will watch a movie for two hours, enjoy a baseball game for three hours, and are mad when it ends because they want more. We will devote ourselves for a whole day to clean up our homes but cannot devote ourselves to come to an hour prayer meeting. We must ask ourselves: what are we devoted to?

We are devoted to our jobs. We strive to be on time and push ourselves to out do every one else in hopes of being promoted. One of my pet peeves is when people who get up Monday through Friday to go to work but have the most difficult time getting to church every Sunday and claim they are devoted to the things of God. Now that I've got that out of the way, let's go on. We are devoted to our vehicles. We change the oil every 3000 miles and when the money is right, we even bless our vehicle with supreme gasoline. We pay our car note on time every month and even pay another fee to protect it just in case something happens to our vehicle. It's called insurance in case you missed it. We are devoted to certain relationships. We will drive hundreds of miles in a storm to get to the one we love. I know because I've done it.

I remember my college days. I had two good friends and each of us dated girls who lived in Houston, Texas. The school we attended was in Dallas, Texas, some 300 miles away. Daily we would plan for the next time we would go to Houston to visit our girlfriends. Each of us were members of the football team which made travel hard because the only free time we really had was on weekends when we didn't have games or immediately following a home game. Here was the dilemma. Most of our home games would be on Saturday nights, so once we were through, it would be about 10 or 11 o'clock.

After games we would look at each other and decide whether we would go or not. Often we would be tired, bruised up, it would be raining, but when we thought about what we were going for, we quickly packed our bags and hit the road. Three young men, one was six foot six, the other about five foot nine, and me being five foot seven. You may be asking what did our heights have to do with it? I'm glad you asked!

At the time, only one of us had a vehicle and that vehicle was a small, baby blue Nissan truck. Not an extended cab, but a single cab truck. Those rides were most uncomfortable for me because I was the shortest and the middle was reserved for the shortest person, namely me. Riding three hundred miles between a defensive end and an outside linebacker felt like I was trapped in a can of sardines. The only time I was comfortable was when I was driving.

As I look back on those road trips, I recall that it often rained on our journey. The defroster did not work most of the time and we would have problems with the windshield wipers on occasion. On top of all this the truck would break down, but regardless of how uncomfortable we were, regardless of the length of the trip, we were determined to get to our girls. Now you may say that you guys were just crazy. You're right! We were crazy. We were crazy in love with our girls and were committed and devoted to do anything to get to them. My question to you is how crazy are you for the things of God? Do uncomfortable situations cause you not to fulfill obligations? Does a little rain cause you to stay home from church when you have driven through storms to get to work? The determination and devotion we exert in other things should not surpass our determination and devotion in the things of God, but let the weather man say on Thursday there's a 30% chance of rain for Sunday, we make up our minds we are not going to church on Sunday. Well, maybe you don't do that, but I'm sure you know someone who does. We need to become crazy devoted to the things of God. Nothing in our lives should have priority over God and His kingdom. Listen to what Jesus says concerning this crucial issue.

But seek first His kingdom and His righteousness; and all these things shall be added to you (Matthew 6:33, NAS).

Jesus made this statement after addressing the issue of worrying. He was talking to people who were worried for whatever reason about what they would eat, what they would drink and what they would wear. Jesus tells His listeners not to worry and draws their attention to nature. He tells them to observe the birds of the air, how they neither sow nor reap nor gather into barns, but yet God takes care of them. Think with me for a second. When was the last time a bird flew to your doorstep asking for food? Well Jesus says just as I take care of the birds, I'll take care of you as well if you put me first in your life and make my priorities your priorities.

He doesn't just stop with food though. He moves on to clothes. He calls their attention to the flowers of the field and how beautifully adorned they are while never toiling or spinning; and still even Solomon in all his riches could not out dress one of these.

When we make the concerns of Christ our concerns, He in turn takes care of our concerns. If He will feed a bird and I am much more valuable than a bird, and clothe a flower, I know He will take care of me. But we must first devote ourselves to Him.

Another important area of devotion we need to address is the issue of reputation. Often it is the desire to live up to other people's standards of what we should be doing, what we should wear, who we should hang out with that causes us to lose sight as Christians as to who we really are and who we represent. We have become more concerned about what people think of us than what God thinks of us. As God's people we have been called to please Him and in pleasing Him reach the world.

We are therefore Christ's ambassadors, as though God were making his appeal through us (2 Corinthians 5:20, NIV).

As ambassadors for Christ, we represent an entirely different nation. Let me see if I can make this plain. An ambassador functions as the representative of a country. You will never see an ambassador represent more than one country. The ambassador doesn't carry his personal agenda; his agenda is the agenda of the country he represents. In making this commitment of making his country's agenda his agenda, in return, the country he represents takes care of all his needs. When I say all, I mean all.

- Housing.
- Transportation.
- Food.
- Clothing.
- Kid's education.
- Vacations.

All!

In devoting himself to the causes and interest of his country and as a representative of his country, the country is obligated to take care of him. When we realize the power of 2 Corinthians 5:20 and who we are as Christ's representatives, all of our worries will fade away. No longer do I have to worry about my needs being met because my needs are now His responsibility. You may ask why Christ would take on the responsibility to supply my needs. The answer is simple. He doesn't want you pre-occupied with other concerns. He wants your focus to be on His kingdom, reaching the lost, prayer, bible study, preaching, teaching, mentoring to the glory of His name. You can't do these things effectively worrying about what your children are going to eat tonight. You can't represent Him effectively worrying about whether you will have a house to live in or clothes to wear. This is why Jesus tells us to seek His kingdom first and He will take care of our needs. When we take care of God's business, God will take care of ours.

And as if that wasn't enough, we have another privilege as ambassadors. Wherever an ambassador goes, he is protected. If you have ever watched CNN or any news station that covers world events, you will notice that whenever ambassadors travel, they never travel alone. They travel in caravans. They are escorted from destination to destination because the safety of the ambassadors is important to the country they represent. Armed escorts keep a close eye out for any possible signs of danger and it is their duty that no harm befalls the ambassador. Why is this? For it seems that this person is no different than you or me. On the contrary, there is a big difference. The difference is his position and his mission. His position sets him apart from ordinary people and his mission is to be a spokesman for his country to other countries. Get the picture. An ambassador's position and mission make him an important person and it's who he is and what he does that makes it necessary that he be protected at all times.

So it is with Christ's ambassadors. We have a position and a mission as well.

> *But as many as received Him, to them He gave the right to become children of God, even to those who believe in His name (John 1:12, NAS).*

> *Go therefore and make disciples of all the nations, baptizing them in the name of the Father and the Son and the Holy Spirit, teaching them to observe all that I commanded you; and lo, I am with you always, even to the end of the age (Matthew 28:19-20, NAS).*

As children of God, we have a position in the kingdom of God. We are not ordinary people; we are extraordinary because we belong to an extraordinary God. Our position is so treasured by our Father that our safety is a concern to Him. Because of who we are to Him, He has to take care of us. It's His responsibility! What loving parent do you know who does not take the security of their children seriously? Because of that relationship, safety is key, and any loving parent will make sure their child is safe even at the expense of their own safety. Therefore, as we travel from destination to destination representing the kingdom of God, making disciples, baptizing and teaching, just as an ambassador of a country has as his protection the armed forces of his country, so we as Christ's ambassadors have as our protection the kingdom of heaven and its mighty angels. Everywhere we go, we are escorted by caravans of angels whose sole responsibility is to protect the ambassadors of Christ. That's why David said in the 23rd Psalm that "even though I walk through the valley of the shadow of death, I fear no evil; for Thou art with me."

When we do what God tells us to do and say what He wants us to say, we don't have to take responsibility for what we say and do. When people try to accuse you and take issue with you, simply tell them to take it up with the King because you are only the ambassador on assignment. Our main concern must be on the nation we represent, the nation of Christianity. The opinions, the lifestyles of other nations should not influence our way of thinking and our behavior because we have only one agenda and that is to represent our nation and serve our king faithfully. Devote your time, talent, and treasure to God and watch Him take care of you.

Don't believe the Hype

The world's propaganda has influenced us into believing that in order to be successful and enjoy life we must have fancy clothes, perfect figures, enormous bank accounts, large homes, and $50,000 automobiles. When we accept this lie, we devote the majority of our time, talent, and treasure to the pursuit of things. The things we devote our lives to acquire can be taken away in a moment and more often than not we find out that after we have had these things for a while and the newness wears off, they don't seem as important to us anymore. Hear the unusual request of a wise man.

> *Two things I asked of Thee, do not refuse me before I die:*
> *Keep deception and lies far from me, give me neither*
> *poverty nor riches; feed me with the food of my portion,*
> *lest I be full and deny Thee and say, "Who is the Lord?"*
> *Or lest I be in want and steal, and profane the name of my*
> *God (Proverbs 30: 7-9, NAS).*

Have you ever heard anyone make a request like this? I haven't. In the times we are living in where everyone desires to be rich, a request like this is unheard of. Well, maybe the part to keep deception and lies far from me may be requested, but to give me neither poverty nor riches? Wait a minute! I can understand not wanting to be poor, but not wanting to be rich! Who would make such a request and dare show his face in public? I'll tell you who! It was a man who had learned the secret to enjoying life. This man discovered that the only way he could fully enjoy his time here on earth was to learn to be content. What? That's right. The secret to enjoying life here on earth is not in the abundance of things we have, but in being content with what we have. I hear you saying explain that to me because if wanting to be rich and having things is wrong, brother, I don't want to be right!

If you look at the state of our world today with the rich becoming richer and the poor becoming poorer, you will see two extremes at work: poverty and wealth. Everyone wants to be rich and no one wants to be poor. Each extreme is a danger in and of itself according to Proverbs 30:7-9. But what about finding a place between the two to live, for history has shown us that everyone can't be rich and no one desires to be poor. Can we find a place of peace and happiness even when we are not rich or poor? Yes, and that place is sandwiched between being rich and being poor. It is the house of contentment. The reason the author of Proverbs 30:7-9 could make such a request was he discovered that life in the middle of being rich and being poor was the safest place for him. For if he was rich, he ran the risk of forgetting God and if he was poor, he ran the risk of doing things that would bring shame to God's name. I don't believe in this day anyone desires to be poor, so I won't dwell on that side of the spectrum; however, there is an infatuation in the world to be rich. So let me deal with this issue.

In most cases, becoming rich is a tedious process. For those who inherited their riches this does not apply, but for those who are pursuing the goal to become rich, this holds true. There are some who handle being rich very well. Their riches have not clouded their judgment between right and wrong and they are generous with what they have. To these people I give praise to God; but for others, this is not the case.

Through careful observation of people and events, I have noticed three pits on the road to becoming rich that claim pursuers of riches in one form or another.

Relational pit

The first pit on the road to becoming rich is the relational pit. It is at this junction that relationships that should have priority are placed on the shoulder of the road where they eventually drift away into obscurity.

- Fathers who constantly work extra hours in an attempt to become rich at the expense of missing their son's football games.
- Mothers striving to climb the corporate ladder while neglecting the cry for attention from their teenage daughter.
- Pastors in their attempt to expand their ministry endeavors while their own children are wounded, lost, and feel that everyone else is more important to mom or dad than they are.
- Marriages destroyed because there is no time to spend quality time with a spouse. All the time you have is spent at the office, out of town, chasing riches while your marriage is becoming poor.

The list goes on. I have seen this with my own eyes. Those vying to become rich monetarily find themselves becoming poorer and poorer in the area of relationships that matter most.

Spiritual pit

This pit is crucial because it affects who we truly are: spiritual beings. When God speaks to us He does so through our spirits.

- Our spirit man suffers because we work on Sundays and at other times the body comes together in fellowship to learn God's Word. We seldom have time to pray or read our bibles making us insensitive to the voice of God.
- When we are weak spiritually, we conform to the ideas and behaviors of the world and our lives no longer bring glory to God's name.
- We lose sight of who is really in charge of all things. We seek fulfillment in things money can buy only to find ourselves continually buying more and more, never being filled.
- Our goal in life is no longer to get closer to God, but to become rich. Remember what Jesus said, "no man can serve both God and mammon." (Matthew 6:24). Our lives drift away from being God-centered to being self-centered.

Social pit

This pit causes us to lose sight of what's going on around us. With our focus on riches, we become blinded to the needs and concerns of the world around us. We fail to get involved in the lives of others and the majority of our time is spent calculating our next move on the road to becoming rich.

A few passages from the New Testament show the extents Jesus went to help people. In each of the passages the message is clear that Jesus never was caught in a compromising position and he never stooped to the level of those he sought to help. It was always his intention to raise their level of consciousness so they could believe on him and follow him.

John 4:3-10 is the story of Jesus talking to the Samaritan woman at Jacob's well. This incident in the life of Jesus speaks to the fact that Jesus went to a place to minister where others refused to go. The Samaritans were viewed as an impure people and therefore the Jews of that day did everything they could to avoid traveling through Samaria. Cultural differences and places of residence did not hinder Jesus in his mission to seek and save the lost. Jesus dared to go where others refused to go.

In Mark 2:15-17, Jesus associates with wicked people. The religious leaders of the day were of the opinion that they should not associate with such people. However, Jesus says,

> *Healthy people don't need a doctor--sick people do. I have come to call sinners, not those who think they are already good enough (Mark 2:17).*

Jesus did not discriminate. His desire and mission were to help all he could and make those who others considered scum feel comfortable enough to sit at his feet to be blessed. The sick, downtrodden, abused, tax collector, and the adulteress all found deliverance in him. Jesus showed himself friendly and made himself available to the sinner.

In Mark 2:23-24, Mark 3:1-2 and Luke 14:1-6 the issue of tradition is confronted. Many of the religious rulers were so caught up in their rules and regulations that they lost sight of what was good and right. Jesus implied in Mark 3:4 that there is no set time to do good. Jesus went outside the box of tradition to help people.

The last point addresses Jesus' handling of two of his disciples: Peter and Judas. John 13:1-5, 11 speaks to the fact that in spite of the way others will treat Christians, they must still be willing to love and serve them. As Jesus washed his disciples' feet, verse 11 says he knew who would betray him, referring to Judas. The text also states Jesus knew Peter would deny him. Christians are not given particular insight into the downfalls of the other ten disciples; however, the author concludes that Jesus knew what their struggles were also. Knowing their doubts and shortcomings, Jesus still ministered to them. When we are in the social pit, the following are evident:

- We place our wants ahead of the needs of others.
- We forget where God brought us from and if it had not been for His grace and loving-kindness we could be in the same condition as those homeless and hungry.

Whenever our desire to be rich is given priority in our life, we will end up poor in areas of our lives that will not only affect us, but will affect those we care about the most.

Chapter 5

What Matters Most

Understanding the mistakes of the past is what allows us to advance as a society. As the church of the 21st century, we must analyze the mistakes made back in the early church, and resolve not to make those same mistakes. It's time to go to another level in God and we cannot go unless we tighten up some of our loose ends. One mistake or loose end that stands out in the early church is the tragedy that occurred in Acts 5. You know it all too well. It is the story of Ananias and Sapphira.

> *But a certain man named Ananias, with his wife Sapphira, sold a piece of property, and kept back some of the price for himself, with his wife's full knowledge, and bringing a portion of it, laid it at the apostles' feet. But Peter said, "Ananias, why has Satan filled your heart to lie to the Holy Spirit, and to keep back some of the price of the land?" (Acts 5:1-3, NAS).*

As we read the book of Acts, all is well with the church until Acts 5. In chapter one we witness the promise of the Holy Spirit. In chapter two we witness the fulfillment of the promise on the day of Pentecost. In chapter three we witness the healing at the temple of the lame beggar by Peter and John. And in chapter four we witness the boldness of men who are confident in what they have heard and seen.

There is unity among the believers. There is honesty, sharing, caring, and excitement because of the way God is blessing the church. When we operate in this realm, the power from heaven empowers us to be what God ordained us to be; the hope of the world. Although outside forces were mounting attacks against the infant church, the church itself remained undaunted. Lives were being changed. People were being healed and delivered from their lives of hopelessness and despair. Yes, the church had it going on! But isn't it strange that when we are advancing to the mountain top, someone or something is always there to try to derail us. Life has a way of throwing us off track when we take our focus off what truly matters most and place it on temporary wants and pleasures. Instead of serving to serve Christ, we serve to be seen and praised of men. Instead of loving just because, we love to be loved in return. Sometimes the people we love will not love us back- ask Jesus!

It is during the times when great progress is being made that we must be careful not to let our guards down. In the face of great progress there is always great resistance. It is inevitable! We should not be surprised when it comes, we must be prayed up because our adversary is always looking for a crack where he can slip in and in Acts 5, he found one.

For The Love of Money

When we look at some of the challenges we face in the church today, most of them center around one thing- money. It may be that the members of a particular church are not giving what belongs to God out of a lack of trust in Him. Others may have a lack of trust in the leadership so they don't give in fear of their money being used for things not connected to the kingdom. Still others have never truly been taught the biblical reasons why they should give and as a result, frustration and discord sets in because those who know the biblical principles of giving and practice them assume everyone else knows them, and many who don't know are waiting to be taught. Whatever the case may be in your particular church, pray that God will reveal it to the leadership and lead them to deal with it from the word of God.

For some, addressing the giving of money in the church is a sticky situation. When the issue arises, many Christians turn a deaf ear to the leadership. At one time in my ministry I decided never to talk about or preach about giving to church people because every time I did, they would get upset and say things like, "all the church talks about is money", and "I'm not giving my money to that preacher. He drives a better car than me and lives in a bigger house than me." Well, after you have been bombarded with statements like these over and over again, they sort of wear you down to the point you lift up your hands and say, what the heck!

However, one night as I was reading Acts 5, the Holy Spirit spoke a word in my spirit that took away my reservations of talking about money. From Acts 1 to Acts 4 the church was running smoothly and along came chapter five and the first problem- And what was the issue centered around? You guessed it! The one thing even today we don't want to hear about in church-- money. When I saw that, my thinking was immediately changed on the subject because whether we want to admit it or not, money is important to us. When it comes to our priorities in life, our lips say God, family, health, church, and then money. But our lifestyles and obedience to God show money, health, family, church, and then God. It's no coincidence that the one thing we don't want to hear about in church is the one thing we are clinging to the most. Yes, money matters to us. Not just a little; money matters a lot! We need money. Money is good to have. However, we as the people of God must have the proper attitude towards money. Paul gives us a piece of advice on this issue.

> *And if we have food and covering, with these we shall be content. But those who want to get rich fall into temptation and a snare and many foolish and harmful desires which plunge men into ruin and destruction. The love of money is the root of all sorts of evil, and some by longing for it have wandered away from the faith, and pierced themselves with many a pang (1 Timothy 6:8-10, NAS).*

What happened in Acts 5 gave Satan an entry port and the church has struggled in this area ever since. It's alright to have money, but when our attachment to money outweighs our devotion to God, Paul tells us in 1Timothy that we are candidates to fall into temptation and our own desires will destroy us. If my desires are fueled by my quest to become rich, my desires become harmful and lead to a dangerous path that only ends in destruction. Marriages have been destroyed over money. Friendships have been lost over money. Families have been ruined behind someone's unhealthy attitude towards money. That's why Matthew 6:24 says "no one can serve two masters; for either he will hate the one and love the other, or he will hold to one and despise the other." What a statement! He will hate the one and love the other. Hold on to that because it is key!

We must be careful in interpreting this passage because often it (1 Timothy 6:10) is quoted as "money is the root of all evil." The bible doesn't discourage us from having money, on the contrary, it encourages us to work for it and use it wisely. Money is used as an exchange for goods and services. Without it we would not be able to buy food, shelter, and other necessities of life. The misuse of this scripture has led some to criticize and even dislike those who in the course of their toil have become financially secure. As long as the person keeps God at the forefront of their life and not money, we should praise God for their success and be happy for them. Too often we become bitter and hateful because our own desires of becoming rich have not materialized and we are jealous of the success of others. Don't be jealous, simply continue to put God first in your life and He will supply all of your needs according to His riches in glory.

Paul gives us the reason why we should not allow ourselves to fall in love with money. He tells us that "some have wandered away from the faith and have even inflicted pain on themselves" (1 Timothy 6:10, NAS).

A Thin Line

We teach our kids to never talk to strangers. In the times we live in, people are luring children into vehicles and isolated areas to molest them and even kill them. It seems that every time we turn on the news we hear of another abduction. Enticed by an offer of ice cream or candy, many children have taken the bait and been captured by evil- minded men and women whose sole purpose in life is to violate and injure little children. Our enemy knows what to entice us with. If he can get us to take the bait, he has us right where he wants us. Too often, we as Christians have taken the bait of falling in love with money and in doing so, the kingdom suffers as well as our souls.

There is a particular word in Matthew 6:24 that at times has been misunderstood. That word is hate. When we hear the word hate, we often think of a person we strongly dislike, or a food we despise. When we think of hate, we think of negative emotions directed at a person, thing or idea. But in Matthew 6:24, Jesus is not saying that we would hate God in the sense of despising Him. Let's look at another familiar passage that brings this word hate into focus.

If anyone comes to Me, and does not hate his own father and mother and wife and children and brothers and sisters, yes, and even his own life, he cannot be My disciple (Luke 14:26, NAS).

Why would Jesus tell us to hate our mother and father when we are commanded to love, honor, and obey them? Why would He tell us to hate our wives men when we are commanded to love our wives as Christ loved the church? Why is He telling us to hate our children, our brothers and sisters, and even our own lives? He can't be saying what it sounds like He is saying. Guess what, you're right. He is not saying what you think He is saying.

When the word hate is mentioned in Matthew 6:24 and Luke 14:26, it is not referring to hate in our usual sense of the word. The term here for hate is the Greek term miseo, which means "to love less." When we understand the meaning of the word, the scriptures become clear. We are not to despise money and view poverty as something we should aim for, but we should not place a higher value on money than our love and relationship with God the Father, Jesus the Son, and the Holy Spirit our comforter and guide. When He says hate mother, father, children, sister and brother, He is saying no other relationship should be valued above our relationship with Him. Get the picture? Anything in your life that you value or love more than God is your god, and that thing, idea, or person, you will serve and worship. What matters most to you in your life right now?

Concerning this issue, God told the Israelites in Exodus 20:4-6 that they should not worship idols or serve them because He is "a jealous God, visiting the iniquity of the fathers on the children, on the third and fourth generations of those who hate Me" (love Me less), "but showing loving-kindness to thousands, to those who love Me" (love Me more) "and keep My commandments." Our lifestyles, attitudes, choices, and acquaintances are all signs that show us what we value the most. Take a look at your life and checkbook and determine if you value money more than God? Do your choices suggest you value your opinions more than the Word of God? Do your relationships with other people mean more to you than God? If this word is speaking to you, fall on your knees right now and ask God to forgive you for not giving Him first priority in your life.

Devote your life to Him and His kingdom. Make what matters most to Him priority in your life and you will begin to experience the promise of Matthew 6:33; "and all these things shall be added unto you."

Chapter 6

Totally Devoted

And they were continually devoting themselves to the apostles teaching and to fellowship, to the breaking of bread and to prayer (Acts 2:42).

Those whom Jesus had appointed to be His disciples had a lot to say. They had walked with him, talked with him, eaten with him. They had given up their lives to follow him never sure of what was around the next corner. They had sat at his feet as he taught them. They had sat quietly by and listened to him as he prayed to God the father. They had observed him healing the sick and raising the dead. They were amazed at how he turned around the lives of those ostracized by society and given people new beginnings. He had loved them and invested himself in them and now the time had come to fulfill the mandate –"teach them all that I commanded you" (Matthew 28:20).

Throughout the book of Acts, we are given snapshots of the power of God's word. The teaching of the apostles was centered on three things: the life, death, and resurrection of Jesus Christ, everything else revolved around these three tenants. When this message was proclaimed, lives were changed, bodies were healed, cities were transformed, myths were destroyed, and Christianity spread like wildfire. However, the people did not just listen to the apostles teach, they gave themselves to what the apostles taught. They were not just hearers of the word; they were doers also. The issue we face in the church today is moving people from simply being exposed to the word to obeying the word. There is no shortage of preachers; therefore, the problem does not rest with the preaching of the word, it lies with the hearers. Church members are devoted to the choir, the usher board, deacon board and board of elders, but when it comes to being devoted to the word of God, obeying its principles, seeking revelatory knowledge of God's word, this is where we fall short.

When we survey the list of things the early church devoted itself to, the first was devotion to the apostles' teaching.

> *And they were continually devoting themselves to the apostles' teaching (Acts 2:42a).*

This teaching fortified the early church. It brought together people of all races under the banner that Jesus saves. Their teaching inspired fellowship and prayer. It created an expectation for the miraculous and an atmosphere of caring and sharing. Their teaching fostered a lifestyle of consistent cooperate worship and lives of praise. You may say ……….. "all this from teaching the life, death and resurrection of Jesus Christ?" Yes! With this message the whole inhabited world was turned upside down.

But there is something else I must make clear first. We must be careful not to be totally consumed with just learning and studying the word of God. I hear you saying, "you've got to explain that one to me because that sounds off the wall!" Well understand this: If bible knowledge alone could change the world, the world would be a totally different place than it is now because we know more than we've ever known before. People are packing churches every week to learn about the word of God. We know the bible and understand what we should be doing, but all too often it stops there. I am amazed at how many people I come in contact with who have been in the church all their life, and brag about this very fact. Comments such as "I was here when they built this church," "He can't tell me anything, I've been reading my bible since I was a child," or "I've heard that before. When is he going to tell us something new?" What I have discovered is that many Christians are overly educated to the point they are no good to any one else. What they have learned through the preaching of the preacher and other teachings is in their head but has not taken root in their heart where it can find its way into the world to make a difference in people's lives. This may seem gross to you but many Christians are suffering from spiritual constipation. We are stopped up with so much unused information that nothing else can get in. If you have ever been constipated you know it is very painful and you only experience relief when you pass or release that which is stopping you up. I submit to you that if you are spiritually constipated, you need to take some spiritual laxatives. You must begin to use your understanding of the sowing and reaping principle, you must use your knowledge of forgiveness; you must use your understanding of the power of being unified in a common cause. Once you do these things, you will begin to release what had you stopped up and God will be able to invest more into you. You must use what you have before God will give you more. Take a spiritual laxative and get involved. Remember to whom much is given, much is required (Luke 12:48). If you don't release the much that has been given to you, it will cause pain in your life because it was given to you not to hoard, but to pass on. The reason the people were devoted to the apostles' teachings was because they experienced the word working in their daily lives by obeying the teachings and sharing the teachings with others.

If what the apostles taught caused such a transformation then, it would be wise if we not neglect what they taught and devote ourselves to it. Devoting ourselves to what is taught goes beyond simply being able to recite what the preacher said or the three points the teacher highlighted, devoting ourselves to the word means even when others can't read a bible, they can see its message in us. When we devote ourselves to the teachings of the word of God, we act differently than other people. We talk differently. We handle crises differently. Devotion entails giving oneself totally to an idea, person, or thing. What are some things you are devoted to? Is it evident that your devotion to the word of God pails in the face of your other devotions?

What they taught can be summed up in one word: gospel. Paul defines what the gospel is.

> *For I am not ashamed of the gospel, for it is the power of God for salvation to everyone who believes, to the Jew first and also to the Greek (Romans 1:16).*

What the apostles taught was a truth that yielded power. It's impossible to walk in the truth of the gospel and live a defeated life. It's impossible to walk in the power of the gospel and not feel good about yourself. It's impossible to believe in the gospel and not strive to live a life pleasing to the Lord. Once the gospel gets a hold of you, you are never the same. Everyone you come in contact with will notice the difference because you become a different person. People will say I knew him then but you can say look at me now. See what the gospel has done in me, it will do the same thing in you. The gospel is so powerful that when Peter and John were arrested in chapter four and told not to teach the gospel anymore, they replied, "Whether it is right in the sight of God to give heed to you rather than God, you be the judge; for we cannot stop speaking what we have seen and heard" (verses 19-20). The gospel can turn a coward into a warrior. The gospel gives people something to live for as well as something to die for. When I consider the gospel, I am overwhelmed that a holy God would love me so much that He would send His only son to die for a sinner like me. I didn't deserve it, but He did it. I can't repay Him, but yet He still did it. So when I feel like giving up, I can't because the gospel begins to speak to my soul and tells me Christ did not die so I could quit. He died so I could live.

When we accept the gospel, live the gospel, preach the gospel and teach the gospel, we will experience revival in our cities and our world and will see the manifestations present in Acts 2.

Devoted to fellowship

We live in a fast pace society. We go to work or school, we eat, we watch a little television, go to sleep then we get up the next day to do it all over again. In our haste to get things done and to be at certain places, we neglect one important thing, fellowship. In his book, *The Tale of the Tardy Oxcart*, Chuck Swindoll tells this story: In 1765 John Fawcett was called to pastor a very small congregation at Wainsgate, England. He labored there diligently for 7 years, but his salary was so meager that he and his wife could scarcely obtain the necessities of life. Though the people were poor, they compensated for this lack by their faithfulness and warm fellowship.

Then Dr. Fawcett received a call from a much larger church in London, and after lengthy consideration decided to accept the invitation. As his few possessions were being placed in a wagon for moving, many of his parishioners came to say good-bye. Once again they pleaded with him to reconsider.

Touched by this great outpouring of love, he and his wife began to weep. Finally Mrs. Fawcett exclaimed, "O John, I just can't bear this. They need us so badly here."

"God has spoken to my heart, too!" he said. "Tell them to unload the wagon! We cannot break these wonderful ties of fellowship."

This experience inspired Fawcett to write a hymn. "Blest be the tie that binds our hearts in Christian love! The fellowship of kindred mind is like to that above."

The writer of Hebrews says it like this, "Let us not give up meeting together, as some are in the habit of doing, but let us encourage one another-and all the more as you see the Day approaching (Hebrews 10:25, NIV)." What we consider fellowship in many cases is nothing more than socializing. When we think of people we socialize with, they are usually people in our same socio-economic class and share the same interests and hobbies as we do. These individuals often have the ability to take care of themselves and the extent of the relationship is centered on having someone to have fun with and do things with. However, the biblical concept of fellowship goes beyond our secular practice of socializing, just look at the bee.

One bee always seems ready to feed another bee, sometimes even one of a different colony. Mutual feeding among bees, which are very social insects, is the order of their existence. The workers feed the helpless queen who cannot feed herself. They feed the drones during their period of usefulness in the hive. Of course they feed the young. They seem to enjoy the social act.

Bees cluster together for warmth in cold weather and fan their wings to cool the hive in hot weather, thus working for one another's comfort.

When swarming time comes, bee scouts take out to find suitable quarters where the new colony can establish itself. These scouts report back to the group, executing a dance (as they also do to report honey) by which they convey the location of the prospective home to the colony. As more than one scout goes prospecting and reports back, the bees appear to entertain the findings of all scouts and at last the entire assembly seems to reach a common conclusion on a choice. Thereupon they all take wing in what is called a swarm.

When referring to a swarm of bees, swarm means a large number of bees, together with a queen bee, moving together to start a new colony. When referring to people, a swarm is a large number of people in motion. I believe it is safe to say that the body of Christ can be classified as a swarm. We are a large group of people and we are in motion, however, the question is where are we going? Genuine Christian fellowship involves a group of people centered on a common belief in the Lord Jesus Christ moving in the world through love, compassion, dedication, and the message that Jesus is the way.

It is important to note the chronology of things the early church devoted itself to: teaching, fellowship, breaking of bread and to prayer. The fact that fellowship is listed second suggests its importance in the life and welfare of the church. Fellowship is more than a hand shake or a hug and I must admit that I am guilty of this very thing. How often have I shaken a brother or sister's hand without even knowing who they were or even taking the time to find out? This happens in almost every church because in our haste to do, and in some cases not to do, we fail to realize the importance of fellowship. Fellowship is more than getting together. It is more than putting some meat on the grill and talking about old times or gathering the congregation at the nearby park for the annual church picnic. Fellowship is what brings a body closer together. Fellowship helps us to learn about each other and grow with one another. Fellowship gives us access into one another's lives and strengthens our relationships. We must incorporate true fellowship within our local bodies because without it, we are nothing more than a group of people who happen to attend the same church.

The Greek term for fellowship is koinonia where we get our words common, community and commune. Fellowship is the emptying of the believers' hearts to benefit other believers and non-believers with spiritual blessings and material blessings. This word goes far beyond what we do in socializing because koinonia requires me to share in a single life with others with our common focus being God the Father and His Son our Lord and Savior Jesus Christ.

What was from the beginning, what we have heard, what we have seen with our eyes, what we beheld and our hands handled, concerning the Word of Life- and the life was manifested, and we have seen and bear witness and proclaim to you the eternal life, which was with the Father and was manifested to us-what we have seen and heard we proclaim to you also, that you also may have fellowship with us; and indeed our fellowship is with the Father, and with His Son Jesus Christ. And these things we write, so that our joy may be made complete (1 John 1:1-4, NAS).

Our fellowship is not based on prestige. Our fellowship cannot be based on social class. Our fellowship cannot be based on the excitement of our worship services. When true fellowship is in place, it is a result of our fellowship with the Father and with His Son Jesus Christ. When true fellowship is in place, people share their ability, abundance, and have unlimited accessibility to each other. Isn't that what God has done for us through the life of Jesus Christ and what He is doing now through the work of the Holy Spirit? Because we are children of God, we are given access through our fellowship with Him to share in His ability, His abundance, and the unlimited accessibility to Him. When we are weak, His power strengthens us to do what we thought we could not do. When we have not, He makes a way and supplies all of our needs according to His riches in glory. And when we feel all alone and everyone else is so busy with their own lives and issues that they don't have time for us, He is always there willing, waiting, and able to comfort and guide us.

When comparing socializing to fellowship, the people I socialize with do not have unlimited access to me. The truth of the matter is we don't expect that from one another. There are sometimes when I just don't want to be bothered. This is not to say that I hide from them per se, but the things that bond us together are not as strong as the person that bonds me together with my brothers and sisters in Christ. The bond we have with our brothers and sisters in Christ is what makes us get up at 2 a.m. to talk to a brother who is having marital problems or that teenager who is confused about life. You want to know how to evaluate a church, study its fellowship and you will find out everything you need to know.

We are first introduced to the biblical idea of fellowship in Acts 2:37-47. Can you imagine the excitement in the atmosphere as the early church became a loving, caring, and sharing community of faith? People's needs were being met. No one experienced lack. Outsiders were compelled to ask what's going on as they observed the power of true fellowship. If our fellowship doesn't cause the world to take notice of us, we are on the wrong track! If we do not take care of our own, what can we offer those on the outside looking in?

> *And the congregation of those who believed were of one heart and soul; and not one of them claimed that anything belonging to him was his own; but all things were common property to them. And with great power the apostles were giving witness to the resurrection of the Lord Jesus, and abundant grace was upon them all. For there was not a needy person among them, for all who were owners of land or houses would sell them and bring the proceeds of the sales, and lay them at the apostles feet; and they would distribute to each, as any had need (Acts 4:32-35).*

Just reading this passage brings joy to my soul. We must pray that the community of faith would once again become this type of body. The power manifested by the early church was a result of their devotion to the apostles teaching and their devotion to one another. The world is looking for this picture, let's give it to them.

Genuine fellowship allows people to be themselves. When people move into a new community from another city or even from the same town, they need friendship with other people. We all need friendships. People look for churches where there are friendly people. People don't stay at churches because of the preaching. People don't stay at churches because of the singing. People stay at churches because of relationships. We must be mindful that the relationships we have within our churches are centered on our commonality in Jesus Christ. Some people would have you to believe with their cold stares and nonchalant attitude that they are fine by themselves, but when it really comes down to it, they need others just as much as the next person. Fellowship in the church does this.

Devoted to prayer

Recently I noticed a trend at my church when it came to times of corporate prayer. When it would be announced that we were having prayer meeting, people would not show up. So we decided to just schedule it and let the people find out when they arrived. What a shock it was to see people drive 20 or even 30 miles to church, discover the service had been set aside for prayer, and see people walk out in frustration, get back in their cars, and go home. The comments ranged from "Oh, it's just prayer meeting," or "I wish I would have known we were just gonna pray, I would have stayed home."

When it comes to prayer, the attitudes I have experienced in many believers leads me to believe that the devotion to prayer held in previous generations is vanishing and we must somehow rekindle that passion and longing to commune with God consistently through individual and corporate prayer. One way I believe this can be done is by leading and encouraging people to develop a life of prayer. Teaching them that prayer is more than just telling God all about our problems and wants, but telling God how we feel about Him through worship and thanksgiving, and being quiet long enough to listen to what He has to say in response to their prayers.

Everyone loves to be an invited guest. The fact that someone thought enough about us to join them in a time of enjoyment and refreshment lets us know that we are cared for. The child who is invited to a birthday party rejoices at the invitation. The couple invited to a wedding is proud to be a part of such a glorious occasion. How we all love to be invited. Well, if we can get excited about the invitations people extend, how about the invitation God extends to us. It's a personal invitation with your name on it. This invitation lets us know that our heavenly Father cares about us and wants us to enjoy times of enjoyment and refreshment with Him. I believe you would agree in the times we are in we could all use some enjoyment and refreshment in God. In essence, that is what God calls us to in Jeremiah 33:2-3. The prophet finds himself in prison for speaking for God. Life seems to be crumbling around him. He feels alone. There is no one to talk to and in comes an invitation with Jeremiah's name on it that says:

Thus says the Lord who made the earth, the Lord who formed it to establish it, the Lord is His name, 'Call to Me, and I will answer you, and I will tell you great and mighty things, which you do not know.'

What an invitation! The Lord himself invites a man to a time of enjoyment and refreshment. The invitation extended to Jeremiah is extended to us as well because God is not a respecter of persons. What He has done for others, He will do for you. Never again can I feel alone, neglected or insignificant because I have an open invitation from the King of Kings to call on Him and when I do, He assures me that He will answer. Never a busy signal! I don't have to leave a message and hope that He will call back.

My family has set a goal to pray together every night before bedtime. Each of us has a night to lead the family in prayer and I know it has brought us closer as a family. My two boys understand the power of prayer and that God will truly answer our prayers. But there was one thing that was brought to my attention as my kids prayed. In their prayers, they would say "I pray for mommy and daddy," "I pray for my school," "I pray that you would bless the world," you get the picture. Although they were praying, they were not being specific in their prayers. If we are not specific in our prayers, how will we know that God has answered us? Here are a few ways to get your family and church devoted to prayer.

1. **Make prayer a priority – Never let a day go by without praying.**
2. **Be specific in your prayers.**
3. **Pray the promises of God.**
4. **Chart answered prayers.**
5. **Pray for others.**
6. **Pray about everything.**

A particular verse that always gives me hope and assurance when I pray is Ephesians 3:20 which says, "Now to Him who is able to do exceeding abundantly beyond all that we ask or think, according to the power that works within us (NAS). What an awesome praise Paul gives God in these words! Not only does he give God a high praise, but he takes the limits off my mind on how and what I should pray for. Let me see if I can make this clear.

As a father of two young boys, making them tough is important to me. Because of that, I constantly wrestle with them and box with them. When we are boxing, often I will get them riled up by saying "hit me harder", "is that all you've got", and my favorite one, "come on, give me your best shot." You may ask what does your wrestling and boxing with your kids have to do with prayer and Ephesians 3:20. Well Paul lets me know that there is nothing I can ask God to do that is too hard for Him. There is nothing I can think of that He can't perform. When I understand this, my prayers turn into something altogether different. I began to stop just asking God for what I have heard others ask Him for and start asking Him for things I have never heard anyone ask Him for. However, my asking is predicated on the fact that I have the mind of Christ and all that I ask for is directly tied to the advancement of the kingdom of God.

One man asked God for something that had never been asked before. His story is found in the book of Joshua.

> *Then Joshua spoke to the Lord in the day when the Lord delivered up the Amorites before the sons of Israel, and he said in the sight of Israel, "O sun, stand still at Gibeon, and o moon in the valley of Aijalon." So the sun stood still, and the moon stopped, until the nation avenged themselves of their enemies. Is it not written in the book of Jashar? And the sun stopped in the middle of the sky, and did not hasten to go down for about a whole day. And there was no day like that before it or after it, when the Lord listened to the voice of a man; for the Lord fought for Israel (Joshua 10:12-14, NAS).*

Joshua prayed a crazy prayer. *Lord, stop the sun.* Joshua and the nation were running out of daylight in the fight against their enemies so Joshua prays that the sun stay where it was to give them light until the victory was won. What a request! Lord, stop the sun. I believe that God desires us to pray prayers that will go beyond what we can even ask or think. In his asking of God to stop the sun, Joshua recognized that there was nothing too hard for God. Let's begin to give God our best shots in prayer. Pray not only that your family be saved, but pray that your family and their friends and their families and friends be saved. Pray that you will have enough to be a blessing to every needy person you come in contact with. And when we begin praying *stop the sun prayers,* we will soon see God doing even more than we asked Him to do and even those things our minds were not capable of conceiving.

Devoted to evangelism

Acts 1:8 is a principle that broadens the scope of the Christian's ministry and message. Today, the church seems to be content on ministering to those within the confines of the church. Evangelism in many churches has been relegated to a one-time event each month while it should be done on a daily basis through words and lifestyle. Christians have become comfortable in sharing the gospel message to the fish that are in the safety of the aquarium and are neglecting the fish in the rivers and oceans of the world. Christians must first minister where they are. Christians must minister to their families, neighbors, co-workers, and immediate circles. These arenas may be viewed as the Christian's Jerusalem as seen in verse eight.

Christians must also go into places they are familiar with. Judea was a place of familiarity to the first Christians. Places of familiarity may include grocery stores, shopping malls, ball games, and schools. The principle of Acts 1:8 begins with witnessing first at home and branching out.

Christians must go where they do not want to go. Samaria was not a place that many early Christians cared to visit. There are places today Christians care not to go. However, Christians must realize they are the salt of the earth and without salt, this earth will spoil. Countless numbers of people are spoiling in nightclubs, gambling establishments, drug houses, and others. Christians must take on the attitude Jesus Christ displayed when he left heaven to come to a corrupt earth to save people who did not deserve to be saved.

Christians must also go where they have never been (to the ends of the earth). There will be times Christians will be afraid, but the church must dare to share the message of salvation everywhere. The bottom line is Christians must go and stand for truth in spite of!

The church must be known for its stand that the message it preaches will in no way be compromised. Christians must also never let the world silence their witness. In Acts 4:17-20, Peter and John were told by the high council never to speak in the name of Jesus again. However, because of their resolve not to compromise what they had seen and heard they refused to be silenced by anyone and they kept preaching the message of salvation that comes only through Jesus Christ. The church must be willing to suffer persecution and stand on the message that Jesus is the only way to the Father.

I believe the church must begin to pray for the lost in such a way that cannot be paralleled to any other time in history. Romans 10:1 tells of Paul's longing to see God's people saved. This was Paul's sincere prayer. The church prays for everything under the sun. It prays for physical healing, jobs, cars, prosperity, new buildings, but do we pray enough for the salvation of the lost? Christians must place the salvation of the lost on the top of their list of things to pray for. The mission of the church is found in 2 Corinthians 5:18, "God has given us the task of reconciling people to him." This task cannot be accomplished without fervent and consistent prayer for the lost.

Chapter 7

The "Awe" –someness of our faith

And everyone kept feeling a sense of awe; and many wonders and signs were taking place through the apostle (Acts 2:43, NAS).

In order for a man, woman, boy or girl to be enthusiastic about anything in life, there must exist a confidence that what they are involved in and giving their time to is worthwhile. I pay $20-50 to watch a professional football game because I feel it's worth it. I like football. I enjoy the excitement of the game. I savor the fact that at any given time something historic can happen. A running back may run a 99-yard touchdown. A desperation Hail Mary pass can be thrown with two seconds left on the clock to win the game. I love that feeling and when I leave, I talk about the game with others who witnessed the same game with me and with others who did not see the game. The issue is this: things that we feel are worthwhile, necessary, and have a lasting effect on us, we give ourselves to wholeheartedly and will in most cases do whatever it takes to be a part of the experience. Well, maybe you are not a big sports fan like me but there are certain things in your life you deem as necessary, worthwhile, and have a lasting effect. If those things should ever lose their appeal and benefit, your perspective of these things change from worthwhile to a waste of time; from necessary to unnecessary; from having a lasting effect to only producing temporary satisfaction. When this happens, what we once felt we needed is tossed to the side as unnecessary.

I suggest to you now that in the minds of many people, the state of the church today in some arenas has made it "unnecessary" to the masses. Church attendance is down. To say church and commitment in the same sentence is almost obsolete. People are moving from one church to another searching for a place with necessary, worthwhile, and lasting ministry and fellowship that they are willing to commit to for the long haul come rain or shine. We must begin to see the church for what it is: a place where broken people can come and be made whole. That's our duty and when we make our duty the top priority, we will always be necessary. Churches are closing daily. Why? Anything that does not meet a need is unnecessary. The only way to prevent genocide is to become necessary. The church has to become necessary.

A Necessary Church

Acts 2:43 is a powerful verse. In it we see the power of the Holy Spirit at work in the early church. The church was a place for everyone; the Jew and the Gentile, the sick and the healthy, the rich and the poor, the young and the old, the learned and the unlearned. No matter what your issue was, the church was the place that accepted everyone just as they were, but never left them the same.

It was from this atmosphere that the church grew and became a necessary part of human existence. When hurting people witnessed others with their same affliction being set free, they wanted the same for themselves. Therefore, when the question was asked what must I do and where can I go, the response was his name is Jesus and He is moving through a body called the church. The evidence of changed lives was more than enough to fan the flames that gave rise to the spreading of the gospel and the building of the church throughout the world. The healing of the sick through the church left people speechless. Being a part of a group that loved you for who you were and not for what you had gave birth to countless people who committed their lives to the spreading of the gospel and the building of the church.

These people witnessed first-hand the power of the gospel change even the stoniest of hearts and they had to tell it no matter what! What excitement! What happiness! What peace! When we see the early church from this perspective, it is no wonder it grew the way it did. In describing the atmosphere of the early church, Luke says:

*And everyone kept feeling a sense of awe; and many
wonders and signs were taking place through the apostles
(Acts 2:43).*

What worked then will work today and we must rekindle that
same atmosphere. *We need a sense of awe.* Luke says they kept
feeling a sense of awe. There was always something that kept them
aware of the power of God and they experienced it together as a
community of believers. It was not just the healing of physical
ailments that kept them feeling a sense of awe, I believe there were
several other factors present.

During a bible study series my pastor taught on giving, he
challenged the church to bring something of value, something
that we really wanted to keep for ourselves and give it away. The
people responded and what a glorious time we had in the Lord on
that particular night. Never before had the church experienced a
sense of awe like that before. People who were in need of clothing,
babysitters, watches, perfume, money, whatever you can think of,
received on that night just what they were in need of or had a desire
for. People who had normally watched the clock with anticipation
of going home were in no hurry to go home that night. When the
benediction was given, hardly anyone left. People were gathered
around praising God and rejoicing over what had just occurred. Days
went by, weeks went by, even months and people were still talking
about that night. What joy the church felt! From that day there was a
new-found excitement that was in the church. As I reflected over the
event, the Holy Spirit said this should not be out of the ordinary, this
should be the norm. What we had experienced on that Wednesday
night was what everyone kept feeling in Acts 2:43, a sense of awe.

We feel a sense of awe every now and then. We say awesome
when there are no words available to describe what we saw, heard,
or felt. It's the word in our vernacular that we use to describe God.
When we try to describe the works of God, the love of God, His
forgiveness and all He does for us, all we can say is our God is
awesome. Even though we use this word to describe athletic events
and other emotional experiences, this word truly and only applies
to God. The word awe or awesome is defined as a mixed feeling
of reverence, fear, and wonder, caused by something majestic,

sublime or sacred. (Webster's New World Dictionary, Third College Edition)

Our English word awe comes from the word *phobos,* which means a godly fear capable of a good interpretation. The experience we had that Wednesday night was capable of a good interpretation and the interpretation was the church is much more than what it has become. When we reverence God for who he is and obey what he commands, His grace and love will be showered on us in such a way that when we leave our worship experiences, all we will be able to say is awe!

But how often do we leave our worship experiences with a sense of awe? More often than not we leave with a sense of guilt, frustration, disappointment and even contempt. I believe the church is experiencing this area of downfall because it is focusing on the wrong things. When we focus on the things of God and place our personal and self seeking ambitions and desires on the back burner, God receives glory from our lives and the body is edified. But when every one is looking out for "numero-uno" and only has what they desire and their selfish ambitions as their goals, then no one is edified and the body suffers greatly. Instead of feeling a sense of awe, we feel a sense of "why am I a part of this in the first place?"

When we leave a worship experience the one thing in our mind should be I can't wait to come back! One thing that the bible teaches us is that God blesses the church through covenant and community. God's ultimate purpose is to bless the world through the assembly of the called out ones, the church. However, it's sad to say that when many people leave our churches today, they are not thinking about when is the next time they will come but that they will never set foot in this place again.

It is evident that the sense of awe experienced by the early church had a positive effect on the members as well as those on the outside looking in. When those on the outside of the church today look in, what do they see? Do they see love or do they see hate? Do they see sharing or do they see stinginess? Do they see servanthood or do they see everyone doing his or her own thing? Do they see organization or do they see confusion? Do they see honesty or do they see dishonesty? Do they see true worship or ostentatious religious acts? If you have been a part of the church for any length of time, I don't have to answer these questions for you.

When we were little, we would play church. We would form a choir, someone would be the preacher, and the rest would form the congregation. If the act was pretty good, we could keep our audience's attention for quite a while. However, if the show was boring, the congregation would soon lose interest and go back to what they were once involved in. This seems to be the state of the church today. Many are coming but not many are staying. For when a sinner is searching for a place of refuge and peace, he needs to know the place he is in is authentic. What I mean by this is if what people see on Sunday contrasts the everyday life of the people who say they belong to God, then the sinner will never experience or understand what the Christian life is all about. People are not experiencing that sense of awe because our worship has been transformed into theatrical performances to draw the most people with no intent on touching the heart of God. The prophet Amos addressed this issue with the nation of Israel.

> *"I hate, I reject your festivals, nor do I delight in your solemn assemblies. Even though you offer up to Me burnt offerings and your grain offerings, I will not accept them; and I will not even look at the peace offerings of your fatlings. Take away from Me the noise of your songs; I will not even listen to the sound of your harps. But let justice roll down like waters and righteousness like an ever-flowing stream. (Amos 5:21-24)*

The religious climate during Amos' prophesies was one of complacency and hypocritical worship. The rich were becoming richer while the poor were becoming poorer. The people had reneged on their part to love God with all their heart. The name Amos means burdened, and thus God sends a representation of what the people's worship and lifestyles were doing to His heart, burdening Him. There were not a lot of people who liked the prophet. The prophet was the man who talked to the people on the behalf of God. When Amos spoke these words it came as a shock to the hearers. For they believed they were doing what it took to please God. How often have we become so complacent in the things we do that we forget why we are doing them and to whom?

They were attending the religious festivals. They were bringing their offerings. They were singing songs and playing instruments in the name of giving praise and glory to God. Never did they realize that while they were enjoying themselves in these endeavors, God was sitting on His throne saying I hate all that you are doing. You hate what we are doing! What do you mean?

This is what church is all about. It's all about coming to a place where other believers are to sing and shout and enjoy the Lord. That's what we are doing and you say you hate it? Yes, that's what God is saying. Whenever we go through the motions and serve with the wrong motives, whatever we try to do for God goes up as a stench in His nostrils. Whenever we offer up praise and worship from sincere and repentant hearts, God accepts it and allows us to experience Him in such a way that all we can say is awe. When people will participate not only when it's convenient for them and will truly put God first in every aspect of life, the church will experience that sense of awe that made the early church explode into a force that drew millions to the risen savior Jesus Christ. I believe people are looking for more than a good song and a shout. I believe people are looking for more than spectacular buildings. People are searching for a peace that surpasses all understanding. People are seeking a peace that when all hell breaks out around them, they can still have joy and contentment. People want to know what it really means to have a relationship with God, not a relationship with the church.

I am often amazed at the statement, "We had some good church." When this statement is made, it references the singing of the choir or how many people stood up and shouted or ran around the church. When this is experienced, it feels good for a little while, but no change has occurred and no one has really been made any better. Good church is when people experience the transforming power of God. When the Holy Spirit convicts hearts and minds to exercise justice and righteousness, when people are healed, relationships mended, commitments are made and upheld........ that's good church.

The world is looking for God. However, it won't find Him in the midst of theatrical performances. God will not show up where man is not worshiping Him in spirit and in truth. We cannot fool God with our pseudo worship. External exploits do not depict what's in the heart. God wants us to experience Him in a real way just as the early church did.

> *But in your hearts set apart Christ as Lord. Always be prepared to give an answer to everyone who asks you to give the reason for the hope you have (1 Peter 3:15).*

The reason for their hope and steadfastness to endure persecution even until the point of death was based on the fact that they knew God was real. They had seen the resurrected Christ for themselves. We may not see Him as they did in the flesh, but we can experience him in the spirit as we submit ourselves to his Lordship and experience him in our worship and in our sense of coming together as a community of believers. When we set apart Christ as Lord, our lifestyle becomes a testimony to the goodness of our God and the life of His son is lived through us. When we live the Christian life, lives are changed, people are delivered, needs are meet, the impossible becomes possible, maturity takes place, relationships are restored, healing occurs, and in the midst of all this, we experience the sense of awe we should expect because of our obedience to the Lord.

When we experience the sense of awe, it is not God's desire that we only feel who He is, but that we realize our potential in Him. We are shown what God can do to and through a people whose hearts and minds are stayed on Him, but to the end that the sense of awe will indicate the grace and power of the doer himself – God. The purpose of miracles and great wonders in the early church was to produce an ethical end and to demonstrate the purposes of God. We must foster an atmosphere in our churches that creates a sense of expectancy. If we come expecting to see God heal the sick, restore relationships, break generational curses, and add to the body, we must put our faith in action, pray for unity, cooperation, consistency, holiness, and lives yielded to the work of the Holy Spirit. God wants us to experience more of Him in this generation, let's open our hearts to receive what He wants to give us.

Rekindling the awe

There are several things I see in the scriptures concerning the early church that must once again be our basis for staying necessary and relevant in a world that needs hope. The way the church is viewed is crucial. We must be what we proclaim to be. After you have read the items I will present through the power of the Holy Spirit, pray to God personally and see where you are lacking and then have your church to pray corporately to identify where the body is lacking. Pray that God will give you a plan and go to work on rekindling the awe.

1. Rekindle by being a forgiving church.   Jesus said in Matthew 6:14, 15 "For if you forgive men for their transgressions, your heavenly Father will also forgive you. But if you do not forgive men, then your Father will not forgive your transgressions."

We must begin to teach and preach about forgiveness more. The bible says faith cometh by hearing and hearing by the word of God. We must have faith in the power of forgiveness. Not only must we preach it but we must exercise it consistently. Everyone deserves to be forgiven. If Jesus forgave you, who are you to withhold forgiveness to someone else. Forgiveness has delivering power. When you forgive and are forgiven, you are set free to be what you were destined to be. The church is to be a loving community and others should be able to see this. Whenever unforgiveness is present we send out a distorted picture. Those outside say, "if they can't forgive one another I know they won't accept me for who I am and what I have done." Jesus forgives us when we ask with sincere hearts. No matter what we have done, He will forgive us. We must grasp this reality by applying it in our daily lives so there will be no doubt in the minds of others that the church is a place of forgiveness.

The danger of unforgiveness is that it spreads like wildfire and causes confusion and warring factions to arise. Every church should be united as one. Everyone should be on the same page, for where there is unity there is strength and nothing destroys unity like unforgiveness. We don't have time to let differences in opinion cause words to be said and actions to be taken that cause division, but through the power of the Holy Spirit we must forgive and come together to do great things to bring glory to God.

People who feel they have been wronged and do not address the issue with the one they have the issue with usually go and tell someone else. The negative attitude towards the accused person is transferred to another who in many cases does not personally know the individual. When you have a negative perception of someone, you generally don't speak to that person and if you do, it is not from a loving heart. Don't allow other people's perceptions of others cause you to form an opinion about the person without getting to know the person yourself. Stop being a garbage can where others dump their trash about others on you. Many today are holding grudges against someone because of what someone else said or did. We must forgive one another. People are dying in the streets while the church is majoring in unforgiveness. Our children are picking up the bad habit of unforgiveness by watching and listening to us. It must stop now. If you are angry with someone, you probably won't help them. If you have resentment towards a person, you probably won't pray for them other than to say "Lord get him or her." Unforgiveness is a killer of relationships and saps the strength of a church. Start now. If there is someone in your church you haven't forgiven for whatever reason, forgive them and rectify the situation as soon as possible. Let the rekindling process begin with you. Remember, if you don't forgive, your Father will not forgive you. As He cast our sins as far as the east is from the west, let us do the same. Whatever happened in the past, forgive, cast it away, and move on. When others see us forgiving each other for things that seem unforgivable, all they will be able to say is awesome.

Commit this passage to memory and allow it to govern your life and the life of the church you are a part of in the realm of forgiveness: "Therefore, laying aside falsehood, speak truth, each one of you, with his neighbor, for we are members of one another. Be angry, and yet do not sin; do not let the sun go down on your anger, and do not give the devil an opportunity" (Ephesians 4:25-27).

2. Strive to meet every legitimate need. At some point we all will run into hard times. Life has a way of handing us unpredictable situations that we need help to overcome. The church must strive to meet the needs of its members. Members should not be ashamed to ask their church to help meet a legitimate need in their lives. Take note that I say "legitimate." I do not believe a true Christian can eat caviar and escargot everyday while knowing his brother is hungry. Acts 2:44, 45 says "And those who had believed were together, and had all things in common; and they began selling their property and possessions, and were sharing them with all, as anyone might have need.

It takes more than one or two people participating to make this work. Every member must be willing to sacrifice for the good of the body. When each member of the body does his part, needs will be met in such a way that all they can say is awesome. It's not enough to see a brother in need and say I will pray for you, knowing you have been blessed to meet that need. Faith without works is dead. God sends blessings to those He can send a blessing through. We must be willing to sacrifice our wants to satisfy the needs of others.

3. Strive to keep the unity intact. Acts 2:43-47 shows the power of a unified body. As others saw the love the body had one for another, it compelled them to seek the reason for this unusual type of love. The unity displayed by the church opened the hearts of those outside the church to the gospel message and upon hearing the message, they accepted Jesus Christ as their Lord and Savior. The church must do everything possible to bring the unity back. Christians must be slow to anger and quick to forgive. Christians must share to the point that none may be in want who are numbered among them. Christians must become so entangled in love that when the world thinks of the church, it thinks of Jesus.

Speaking to the church at Ephesus, Paul says, "I therefore, the prisoner of the Lord, entreat you to walk in a manner worthy of the calling with which you have been called, with all humility and gentleness, with patience, showing forbearance to one another in love, being diligent to preserve the unity of the Spirit in the bond of peace (Ephesians 4:1-3).

Verse three shares a very special point that we need to investigate here because the issue of unity is important to the success of the church. When speaking on unity, Paul instructs the church to be diligent to preserve the unity of the Spirit in the bond of peace. The NIV says "make every effort to keep the unity of the Spirit through the bond of peace." Our approach to unity must change. When we look at what Paul says about the unity of the church, he describes it as something to be kept not something to be achieved. We already have unity. We are not striving to become unified we must keep what we already have. You can preserve or keep something that you already have. Therefore, our strategy must change from trying to create unity to realizing our unity has already been purchased and sustained through what Christ did on the Cross. Our unity is not based on denominational statements, usher boards, deacon boards, or longevity, it is based on the promise of God spoken through the prophet Jeremiah, "And they shall be my people, and I will be their God; and I will give them one heart and one way, that they may fear Me always, for their own good, and for the good of their children after them (Jer. 32:38, 39). One heart and one way. As the church, our one heart believes that Jesus Christ is the savior of the world and our one way is Jesus our Lord, who speaking of Himself said "I am the way, the truth, and the life, no one comes to the Father, but through Me (John 14:6). You see, our unity is intact and His name is Jesus. We must keep this unity intact through striving to be at peace with one another. We act as if we are each others enemy when we are not. We are all in this thing together. The devil has tricked us into believing church just ain't church without confusion and discord. Can you see how we have been duped? As long as we are fighting, disagreeing, being jealous of others giftings, stifling progress because we were not asked our opinion, then there is no peace. Paul gave us the key to keeping our unity intact. It is peace. When you understand that peace is how we stay unified, you won't be so quick to say what's on your mind. You will think before you speak and if what you were going to say neither edifies the body or the person you are talking to; if what you want to say doesn't edify the person or situation you are talking about, you need to keep it to yourself. **Peace is mostly threatened by the words that come out of our mouths.**

So also the tongue is a small part of the body, and yet it boasts of great things. Behold, how a great forest is set aflame by such a small fire! And the tongue is a fire, the very world of iniquity; the tongue is set among our members as that which defiles the entire body, and sets on fire the course of our life, and is set on fire by hell (James 3:5,6).

We would have more peace if we would listen more than we talk. The old saying is true, *'some people talk to say something, others talk because they have something to say.'* How true this is. If you are a person who believes in saying whatever is own your mind, know that that's not Christ-like. Society has influenced us to the point where people feel they have the right to say and do anything in the name of free speech. If your speech harms another person, if your speech strips someone of their self worth, it's not free speech it's a dangerous weapon. Learn to think before you speak. Exercise discretion. Just because a thought pops up in your mind doesn't give you the right to open your mouth because all of our thoughts are not godly.

We are destroying speculations and every lofty thing raised up against the knowledge of God, and we are taking every thought captive to the obedience of Christ (2 Corinthians 10:5).

All of our thoughts are not God-centered. In the world we live in, our minds are constantly bombarded with images of ungodliness. If we are not careful, those images will consume our minds and dictate our thoughts. Some of our thoughts are self-motivated to enhance our position often at the expense of someone else. Thoughts that stem from selfish motives are not of God. We must recognize these thoughts and take them captive to the obedience of Christ. Every thing we think and say must be filtered through the 'obedience of Christ.' If your thoughts don't line up with the mind of Christ, you have to take it captive. The bible says let this mind be in you which was also in Christ Jesus. If we have the mind of Christ, we won't get jealous of others because Jesus wouldn't get jealous. If we have the mind of Jesus, we will do all we can to help our brothers and sisters in Christ. If we have the mind of Christ, we won't have to be begged to give our time, talent, and treasure. If we have the mind of Christ we will look like Him in our daily walk. The opposite is true for those who claim to be of God but don't have the mind of Christ. When we don't have the mind of Christ, whatever we think, we believe it is right and proceed to speak it and act it out.

> *And just as they did not see fit to acknowledge God any longer, God gave them over to a depraved mind, to do the things which are not proper, being filled with all unrighteousness, wickedness, greed, evil; full of envy, murder, strife, deceit, malice; they are gossips, slanderers, haters of God, insolent, arrogant, boastful, inventors of evil, disobedient to parents, without understanding, untrustworthy, unloving, unmerciful; and, although they know the ordinance of God, that those who practice such things are worthy of death, they not only do the same, but also give hearty approval to those who practice them (Romans 1:28-33).*

Don't let this happen to you. It is not enough to know about the word of God if you don't live it and allow it to govern your thoughts. There are millions of people who know the bible but do not do what it says. God will protect you and lead you when you have the mind of Christ. When you don't, you are subject to do anything.

When speculations arise, we must ask ourselves whether God would be pleased with our thoughts. The truth is when we think these thoughts, the person or people may not know what we are thinking, but God knows.

> *And getting into a boat, He crossed over, and came to His own city. And behold, they were bringing to Him a paralytic, lying on a bed; and Jesus seeing their faith said to the paralytic, "Take courage, my son, your sins are forgiven." And behold some of the scribes said to them, "This fellow blasphemes." And Jesus knowing their thoughts said, "Why are you thinking evil in your hearts? For which is easier, to say, 'Your sins are forgiven,' or to say, 'Rise, and walk'? (Matthew 9:1-5)*

This passage reminds me of a song we sang in vacation bible school as children that said:

> *O be careful little eyes what you see. For the Father up above is looking down with love. O be careful little eyes what you see.*

I would like to add a verse that says;

> *O be careful little mind what you think. For the Father up above hears everything you think. O be careful little mind what you think.*

If you are guilty of having negative thoughts about someone, ask God's forgiveness right now and pray daily for strength to keep your mind on Him. When we all have our minds on Christ, we will be able to maintain the unity within our churches

Genesis chapter 11 is a look at God's Testament to the power of unity:

> *Now the whole earth used the same language and the same words. And it came about as they journeyed east, that they found a plain in the land of Shinar and settled there. And they said one to another, "Come, let us make bricks and burn them thoroughly." And they used brick for stone, and they used tar for mortar. And they said, "Come, let us build for ourselves a city, and a tower whose top will reach into heaven, and let us make for ourselves a name; lest we be scattered abroad over the face of the whole earth." And the Lord came down to see the city and the tower which the sons of men had built. And the Lord said, "Behold, they are one people, and they all have the same language. And this is what they began to do, and now nothing which they purpose to do will be impossible for them (Genesis 11:1-6).*

Because the people were unified, God said that nothing would be impossible for them. What a testimony! *Nothing will be impossible.* Every church has things it wishes to accomplish and in order to do it, the church must live out what it already possess.

I heard a funny joke once about a man by the name of George Washington Carver Booker T. Jones. The story goes that George Washington Carver Booker T. Jones died one day and opened his eyes to find himself standing in line at the pearly gates. As he waited, he saw numerous men and women walking back with puzzled expressions on their faces. Intrigued by what he saw, he asked a passer-by what was going on at the gate. The response came back to George that St. Peter is at the gate and in order to get in you must ask him a question he does not know the answer to. Well, George was a man of limited learning. He knew that there was nothing he could ask St. Peter that he didn't know. But George said I've come too far, worked too hard not to see the pearly gates. So as George approached the gates and admired their beauty, St. Peter requested he ask his question to enter the pearly gates. George responded:

"I know there is nothing that I know that you don't know. I am a man of limited learning. But there is one question that has puzzled me my whole life and I need and answer to. When will church folk come together?" The story says that St. Peter opened the gates and said, "walk right on in". This joke depicts the attitude toward unity in the church. Some pray for it and others believe it will never be. But instead of praying for it, start praying that we will open our eyes to the reality that it is already here.

Chapter 8

What Kind of People Should We Be?

They worshiped together in the Temple each day, met in homes for the Lord's Supper, and shared their meals with great joy and generosity- all the while praising God and enjoying the goodwill of all the people (Acts 2:46,47 LASB).

Be not conformed to this world, but be ye transformed by the renewing of your mind. As a man thinks so is he. We are a royal priesthood. We are the salt of the earth. Be ye not yoked with unbelievers. We are the light of the world. I want to close this book by allowing you to discover what kind of people we should be.

When people talk about the church, whether their comments are positive or negative, the comments are not about buildings but about people. We should not look like or behave as the world does. We have been called out, chosen to make a difference in this world through our lifestyles.

We opened this book with the questions: what is the church? Who is it? Where did it come from? How did it look in the beginning? How does it look now? What was its original purpose? What is its purpose today? We have searched the scriptures to answer these questions and regain our purpose and focus. Up to this point we have dealt with what makes a corporate body reflect the image of God's design and plan for the church. When it comes down to it, those of us who confess Jesus Christ as Lord and Savior are the church. The church is not our buildings or the different denominations present today. When we get to heaven, there will not be a Pentecostal section, a Baptist section, Catholic section, Church of God in Christ section, Presbyterian section nor will there be a Full Gospel section, we will all be members of the body of Christ.

It is not our particular denominations that make the body of Christ strong. It is not our membership sizes that make the body strong. It is not our financial strength that makes the body strong. None of these things matter if the people who make up the body of Christ are not transformed, renewed, spirit filled believers who live like royal heirs to the kingdom of God. There is an old cliché that says "you may be the only bible someone reads." How true this is! People are looking for reasons not to go to church and too many Christians are giving them plenty reasons. Each of us who claim to be Christians must realize that our lifestyle plays a significant part in the effectiveness of the church.

Picture this scene. You are a mother or father sitting alone in your home with God and He says he will give the man your daughter will marry one exceptional quality of your choosing. This man could be very smart, filthy rich, good-looking, unusually strong and athletic, highly creative and artistic, or he could possess extraordinary character. What quality would you choose?

Now suppose you were picking a principal for your child's school, or a business partner, a deacon, choir director, or even a pastor. What quality would you chose? I would pick character every time. When it comes to Christianity, next to our salvation, nothing is more important than personal ethical virtues like honor, integrity, reliability, trustworthiness, and kindness, or to put it all in one word-character. Our word character comes from a Greek term meaning to visibly and permanently mark as by scratching the face of a stone. A person's character is the permanent and visible sign of his or her inner nature. The great theologian Dwight L. Moody said it best, "Character is what you are in the dark when no one is looking, in the secret chambers of the heart."

Power in the world is based on money and influence. If you possess money and influence, your voice is readily heard and sought after in high places. Never mind what the person believes, the money talks. I don't believe the Lord expects us to use the same tactics as the world. It should not be the position of the church to use financial power to gain access into the halls of change in the world. If you take time to study the word of God and how He caused change, it was always through men and women who possessed godly character.

The great hall of faith in Hebrews 11 accounts men and women who through their faith and inner character brought about change to the glory of God. Change is just change when it fails to bring glory to God and has no regard of bringing people closer to God through a relationship with Jesus Christ.

We learn from Abel that we must always give God our best. People of godly character don't think of doing anything less. When it comes to the giving of our time, talent and treasure, godly character causes us to give God our best.

A Reflection of Love

Love is a powerful thing. People are married because of love. Hearts are broken because of love. Wars are fought because of love. Lives are lost because of love. Yes, love is a powerful thing. The late Marvin Gaye said it best, "Love will make you do right when you want to do wrong and love will make you do wrong when you want to do right." Love is a powerful thing. Whenever we say we love someone or something, it is implied that we are willing to give our best to and for that someone or that something. Love is more than saying I love you; love is the doing of the love you feel. One of my favorite gospel groups of all time, Commissioned has this to say about love, *Love isn't love, till you've given it away.* We talk a lot about love in the church but I want to let you know right now, when it comes to true love, the object of our love should receive the best that we have, nothing less.

The sacrifices we make reflect our love. The time we spend and where we spend it reflects our love. The offerings we give reflect our love. Our perseverance reflects our love. Our commitment reflects our love.

Every Sunday morning, we gather in our churches under the disguise of worshipping and praising God. I say under the disguise because it seems that worshipping God is the farthest thing from many churchgoers' minds on Sunday morning. We must understand that Sunday is the first day of the week and not the last. Sunday should be our first fruit offering to God in expectation of what the rest of the week will bring. When we gather on Sunday morning, we should give God our best worship because He deserves it. However, too many of us see Sunday as the last day of the week and come to church as an addendum to the end of a busy week. So when we treat Sunday as the end and not the beginning, we give God what is left and not what is right. We come in and give Him tired praise. We come and give Him a tip instead of the tithe. We come in thinking about what our plans are for the week and never concentrate on Him. We come in with the attitude that our presence in the service is a favor to God. We come in ready to go so we can get on with the next week. If this is your attitude toward Sunday worship and the first day of the week, don't be surprised when all hell breaks loose in your life Monday through Saturday because you started off wrong. Instead of offering to God your best, you are offering your worst.

If you desire to change, I recommend that you commit to give God your best at all times in spite of negative circumstances and emotional valleys. When you can give God your best at all times, you position yourself to live under an open heaven where God can move on your behalf and on the behalf of others as well.

David, as we know, was a man after God's own heart. He sought to please God. Not that David was perfect because we know he wasn't, but when it came to seeking after God's heart, there was none greater. David's love for God is expressed throughout the Psalms. In them we see the love he had for God and his commitment to God. Yes he stumbled at times as we all do and will, but in spite of it all, he still sought to give God the best he had.

Second Samuel gives us a shocking glance into David's heart during a time he had stumbled.

> *And Araunah said to David, "Let my lord the king take and offer unto what is good in his sight. Look, the oxen for the burnt offering, the threshing sledges and the yokes of the oxen for the wood.*

> *"Everything, O king, Araunah gives to the king." And Araunah said to the king, "May the Lord your God accept you." However, the king said to Araunah, "No, but I will surely buy it from you for a price, for I will not offer burnt offerings to the Lord my God which cost me nothing."*

*So David bought the threshing floor and the oxen for fifty
shekels of silver (II Samuel 24:22-24, NAS).*

In the church today we have an offering problem. We are
offering to God things that don't cost us anything. We serve in
ministry only when we have been laid off our jobs and as soon as we
find another job we stop serving because now we have become too
busy for God's work. We must understand that just because we put
something in the offering tray, the church or religious organization
you are a part of may accept it, but that does not mean God accepts
it. God is not interested in the size of our offerings, He is interested
in the condition of our hearts; the "why" behind the "what." Listen
to these words:

> *And He sat down opposite the treasury, and began observing
> how the multitudes were putting money into the treasury;
> and many rich people were putting in large sums. And
> a poor widow came and put in two small copper coins,
> which amount to a cent. And calling His disciples to Him,
> He said to them, "Truly I say to you, this poor widow put
> in more than all the contributors to the treasury; for they
> all put in out of their surplus, but she, out of her poverty,
> put in all she owned, all she had to live on" (Mark 12:41-
> 44, NAS).*

The size of our offering does not impress God. An offering of
a billion dollars is of no more a significance to God than a dollar.
You can be at the church for hours everyday and involved in every
ministry the church has, but if your heart is not in the right place, God
does not accept the offering of your time, talent, and treasure. Seeds
do not yield an increase if they are not accepted into the ground. So
it is with our offerings. If God does not accept them, they will not
yield an increase. When it comes to what we offer God, we impress
God by the size of our heart and not the size of our gift. If your
offering doesn't mean much to you, it won't mean much to God!
Each time we prepare to give God an offering, we should take time
to meditate on what we will give and make sure it reflects our love
toward God. Let's be like David and live in the revelation that we
will not offer offerings to the Lord our God which cost us nothing.

Lives worth Emulating

Enoch teaches us it is possible to live a life that pleases God. He pleased God to the point that he did not see death. When we please God, there will be certain disappointments and tragedies that God will protect us from.

The life of Noah teaches us to adhere to the voice of God and to follow His instructions. God will lead us if we allow Him to. When we adhere to His voice, benefits come to us and our families.

We learn from Abraham to move when God says move. When God spoke to Abraham, he had no clue of what direction to go. His choices were north, south, east, or west, but staying where he was wasn't an option. Too many of us never do anything or go anywhere because we must always know where we are going, but when God says move, your godly character will give you confidence that wherever you end up will be to His glory.

Sarah teaches us impossible does not exist when God is involved. When we find ourselves in situations out of our control, faced with things that have never been done before, our trust in God that He can do anything gives us strength to keep on believing.

Lastly, Moses teaches us about choices. Hebrews 11:24-26 says, "By faith Moses, when he had grown up, refused to be called the son of Pharaoh's daughter; choosing rather to endure ill-treatment with the people of God, than to enjoy the passing pleasures of sin; considering the reproach of Christ greater riches than the treasures of Egypt; for he was looking to the reward." We must choose whose side we are on; either we are on the Lord's side or not and we must not allow anything to come between our commitment to our Lord and Savior.

Here the words of Charles A. Tindley when he wrote this song:

Nothing between my soul and the Savior, naught of this world's delusive dreams. I have renounced all sinful pleasure, Jesus is mine, there's nothing between.

Nothing between like worldly pleasure, habits of life tho' harmlessly they seem, must not my heart from Him ever sever, He is my all! There's nothing between.

Nothing between like pride or station: Self or friends shall not intervene; Tho' it may cost me much tribulation, I am resolved! There's nothing between.

Nothing between e'en many hard trials, tho' the whole world against me convene; Watching with prayer and much self denial, triumph at last, with nothing between.

The chorus of this song should be a daily prayer for us all:

Nothing between my soul and the Savior, so that His blessed face may be seen; Nothing preventing the least of His favor: Keep the way clear! Let nothing between.

Our power and influence in the world stems from who we are in Christ and how we live out our relationship with Him daily. Money can be lost or even taken away. Those who were once close to you may turn away from you leaving you on the battlefield alone. People may try to sabotage your dreams causing you to want to retreat. All of these things may happen, but through it all, there is one thing that cannot be taken away from you, your character.

One of my favorite characters in the bible is Joseph, the son of Israel. Genesis 39:1-10 turns the spotlight on Joseph's impeccable character and demonstrates the power godly character can bring to the life of a Christian and its effect on the world.

Joseph, the favored son of his father Israel, has become an outcast in the eyes of his brothers. The circumstances of Joseph's birth (being born to the love of his father's life, Rachael, who was barren) secured Joseph's place as the apple of his father's eye. His father made him a coat of many colors and the favoritism Israel showed to Joseph placed Joseph on his brothers' hit list.   Sometime later Joseph's brothers plot to get rid of him and finally when all has been said and done they sell him to a group of Ishmaelite traders for twenty pieces of silver. They took him to Egypt where he became a slave in the house of Potiphar. Joseph was destined to become the prince of Egypt, but before he could ascend to this point, Joseph's character had to be put to the test. Everything we are facing today as a church and as individual believers is preparing us and turning the spotlight on our character. Goethe said, "A talent is formed in stillness, a character in the world's torrents." God is forming our character. Through the hardships, pain, and disagreements, we are being tried as Job 23:10 says.

But He knows the way I take; when He has tried me, I shall come forth as gold.

As we examine Joseph's life, we will be encouraged and motivated to become people of godly character who can be used to bring glory to the kingdom of God.

God's school of character development

Someone asked the great theologian C.S. Lewis, "Why do the righteous suffer?" His reply was, "Why not? They're the only ones who can take it." The truth of the matter is we don't like to suffer. We would rather have everything go our way. We would prefer not to be faced with confrontation. We would like not being lied to when the truth would do. All of these things cause us to question whether or not we are on the right road and even question whether it's worth it. Well, I want to assure you that if what you are going through is God ordained it is worth it.

No temptation has seized you except what is common to man. And God is faithful; he will not let you be tempted beyond what you can bear. But when you are tempted, he will also provide a way out so that you can stand up under it (1 Corinthians 10:13).

When we examine the life of Joseph, the suffering he endured seems unfair. How many times have you been betrayed by those closest to you, falsely accused, stripped of what rightfully belongs to you, or even punished for something you did not do? Is it unfair? Sure it is. But who ever said life was fair? As we travel here on earth, we must develop the resolve that in all things God is at work. In unfair circumstances as well as fair circumstances, God is at work. If we accept this truth, no matter what is thrown our way, we can rely on Romans 8:28: "and we know that God causes all things to work together for the good to those who love God, to those who are called according to His purpose."

For the last three years of my life, God has truly strengthened my walk with Him through the life of Joseph. Through this young man's life, my shortcomings have been exposed. Through his life I have gained understanding and wisdom of how to deal with unjust situations, and most of all, Joseph's life has given me the assurance that whatever comes, God is always with me.

> *Now Joseph had been taken down to Egypt. Potiphar, an Egyptian who was one of Pharaoh's officials, the captain of the guard, bought him from the Ishmaelites who had taken him there. The Lord was with Joseph and he prospered, and he lived in the house of his Egyptian master (Genesis 39:1, 2).*

The first lesson we are taught in God's school of character development is that *God is always with us.* No matter where you are or what circumstances you are in, God will bless a person of character anywhere.

Joseph is an Egyptian slave far away from home but we are told "the Lord was with Joseph, so he became a successful man." We are often placed in uncomfortable situations. Places where we are the minority. Places in which we believe our belief system will hamper our advancement. This belief has caused many Christians to settle for less than God's best and conform to the ways of the world. Yes, we may be the minority, so what! The God we serve is the majority. He is in control. There is not a need that we have that He cannot supply. There is not a closed door He cannot open. Wherever we are, God is there. In the boardroom, God is there. In the classroom, God is there. In the halls of justice, God is there. Just like Joseph was far away from home, we often feel the same way. In places where we are the only ones who seem to care about the things of God, He is there. In places where people tell you, "take a stand, we are behind you," but it turns out that you are left out on a limb by yourself, He is there. We've been there haven't we? But God shows us through Joseph's life that no matter where we are, He is with us and not only is He with us, but He has plans for our success.

In a place where it appeared success was not possible, the word of God tells us that Joseph prospered. Take courage in knowing that you don't have to flee from where you are right now even though you can't see any advancement possibilities or any avenues offering you opportunities for success, God can bless you and make you successful right where you are.

Character will set you apart

When his master saw that the Lord was with him and that the Lord gave him success in everything he did, Joseph found favor in his eyes and became his attendant (Genesis 39:1-4).

When Christians live lives pleasing in the sight of God, the world sees it. We live in a world where Christian values are under attack. A country built on Judaoe-Christian values which is now debating the phrase "One nation under God" in our pledge shows how far we have departed from God. However, we can't blame the world for the state of affairs. We, the church, must accept our responsibility as well. Instead of being separate and unique we have become a part of the system that is destroying lives. There is so much unfaithfulness, adultery, unforgiveness, stinginess, division, and cut-throat mentalities running rampart in the body of Christ that there is no clear distinction between the world and "church folk." Church folk can be some of the most dangerous people you'd ever want to meet. Church folk sing of God's amazing grace but accept it only for themselves and don't believe it applies to others. Church folk talk about the importance of prayer but never pray. Church folk understand the importance of the Word of God but never read it. Church folk seek forgiveness but will not forgive others. Church folk love when others accept their ideas but believe only their way is best.

There is competition over who can build the largest buildings or who can attract the most members while we should be competing to see who can win the most souls to Jesus Christ. We must be different. We must be unique. If people can't recognize a difference in you there's a problem.

When we allow Jesus to be the Lord of our lives, which means we don't make a decision without consulting Him, others recognize us as being different and unique and God's favor on your life is seen clearly. People need to see that God is real and that He loves them. We must give them something to wet their appetite; that something is a life that causes them to ask, "why do you do what you do?" When people began to ask this question of us, we will know that our godly character is setting us apart.

Character will promote you

So Joseph found favor in his sight, and became his personal servant; and he made him overseer over his house, and all that he owned he put in his charge. And it came about that from the time he made him overseer in his house, and over all that he owned, the Lord blessed the Egyptian's house on account of Joseph; thus the Lord's blessing was upon all that he owned, in the house and in the field. So he left everything he owned in Joseph's charge; and with him there he did not concern himself with anything except the food which he ate (Genesis 39:4-6).

Everyone is looking for advancement. No one is content to stay where they are when more is possible. We spend years in the halls of education to acquire degrees that will speak for us when promotion time comes. We beef up our resume with volunteer work, fraternity and political associations to be able to drop names of people we know. We attend functions and galas that we really have no interest in so that we are able to network, to see, and to be seen. From early on we are taught it's not what you know but who you know. Well this may be true in the natural world, but when it comes to being promoted in God's kingdom, man has nothing to do with it.

The culture that we live in has caused us to focus more on the outer appearance of people rather than the inner man. We applaud riches over honesty. It doesn't matter if he has my best interest at heart because he has money. Many have found out in marriages that all the money in the world can't replace a relationship grounded in honesty. You may be able to buy all the clothes, cars, and other gadgets you want, but none of it can give you peace when your husband comes in late and claims he was in a business meeting and you know he is lying. When tragedies like this strike we understand how important honesty is.

We plan "get it quick" schemes and have no remorse for those who will be hurt and we laugh at honest hard work.

> *Lazy people are soon poor; hard workers get rich (Proverbs 10:4).*

It seems that no one wants to get their hands dirty anymore. Everyone wants to be the boss and this attitude has fostered a generation of people who are not only lazy in corporate America, but are lazy in the things of God as well. We all want to be successful, but we don't want to do what it takes to reach our destination the right way. All success is not good success.

> *The Lord hates cheating, but He delights in honesty. Pride leads to disgrace, but with humility comes wisdom. Good people are guided by their honesty; treacherous people are destroyed by their dishonesty. Riches won't help on the day of judgement, but right living is a safeguard against death. The godly are directed by their honesty; the wicked fall beneath their load of sin. The godliness of good people rescues them; the ambition of treacherous people traps them (Proverbs 11:1-6, NLT).*

It's a shame but the truth is, there is just as much cheating and dishonesty in the church as there is anywhere else. If the church you are attending is a place where cheating is tolerated and dishonesty is allowed, the Spirit of God is grieved in that place and you are probably experiencing the crumbs of God's presence when He wants you to experience the whole loaf. That's what I meant in the previous chapter: God wants us to experience His awesomeness, but we won't if we are cheaters and dishonest people. God dwells where the house is yielded to Him. We can't say we are yielded to him and those on the outside can't trust us and many on the inside don't either. Each of us has a responsibility to ensure that honesty, humility, and right living are the mainstays in our Christian lives. When we live in such a way that people know they can trust in us to do the right thing regardless, promotion will come our way both in the world and in the kingdom of God.

Joseph was a slave in the house of his master Potiphar. It's safe to say that there were probably other men in the house who had been there much longer than Joseph who felt they deserved the position Joseph was given. In comes Joseph, a young man who is not even from Egypt and he is promoted to oversee the affairs of his master. Was it because of Joseph's education? No. Was it because of his financial might? Of course not. Was it because of who Joseph knew? Yes, but not in the sense that we are accustomed to looking at it. Joseph was a stranger in a foreign land with no family ties or longtime friends, but he knew God and God knew him. The relationship Joseph had with God produced an inner character that was clearly seen by Potiphar causing Joseph to find favor in the eyes of his master. When the favor of God is upon you it causes others to help you. God knows what He is doing. In every affair of our lives God is moving and to those who have godly character, He directs their steps in such a way that wherever they are He will place them in positions where He will receive the greater glory. If you are not in the place you long for spiritually; if you are not in the place you desire at home and at work, check your character. For as in Joseph's case, character will put a different color coat on you that no matter how you try to fit in with your brothers, your character elevates you above the mediocre and places you on a platform for others to see the favor of God on your life. It's the favor of God that promotes us. The level of your favor comes from God's confidence that He can trust you. Can God trust you with favor?

People who can be trusted will be promoted. Can you imagine where you would be right now if you were trustworthy? When you are not a trustworthy person, news flies fast. People talk. I'm sure you already knew that though. If you do a good deed, very few will hear about it, but if you commit a dishonest deed, all will know. You may be asking what about longevity? Doesn't that count for anything? Well, you can work for someone for 20 years in the basement, but if they can't trust you, you will never be brought up to the penthouse. When people know they can trust you, they will promote you. Listen believer, we need more saved men and women in politics. We need more Christian lawyers and judges. We need more Christians with godly character in positions where they can hire other people with godly character. We need more godly men and women in leadership in our churches. That's right! We know that there are men and women leading us whose character does not reflect the Savior. Listen, someone else is in your spot right now because God is waiting on you to get right.

That position you've been praying and believing for is yours, but God is not going to give it to you in the state you are in right now. He wants your character in line with His heart because ultimately the reason you will be promoted is not for your benefit alone but to bring Him glory through your position and the lives you will be able to impact for Him. Accept what the Spirit of God is saying to you right now. You are in the right place at the right time and you are the right person for the job, but before God will make a move, He must know He can trust you. We must turn the tide because if we don't, things will only get worse.

This can happen but it starts with each of us. Each of us must make a commitment to God to be better Christians. We must discipline ourselves to be faithful in every area of our lives. We must set the standard. When others come to work late, we must be determined to get there on time. While others are stealing paper, staple guns and other supplies, we must refuse to take anything that does not belong to us. When others fail to give their all, we must be known for giving our best at all times. In that regard, we become trustworthy. But remember, we cannot seek to find favor in the sight of man without first gaining the trust of God. You can start today by making Jesus Lord and Savior of your life. Sacrifice your time, talent, and treasure for Him. Make pleasing Him top priority in your life. Pay your vows. Show up when you have given your word. Involve yourself in a ministry to grow spiritually and to help someone else. When He says speak, speak. When He says go, go. When He says shut up, shut up. When He says give, give! Whatever He asks of you, do it without hesitating. When you know it is God speaking to you, heed His voice, obey, and you will soon realize that in trusting Him with what you have, He will trust you with what He has, and what a wonderful exchange that is!

And it came about that from the time he made him overseer in his house, and over all that he owned, the Lord blessed the Egyptian's house on account of Joseph; thus the Lord's blessing was upon all that he owned, in the house and in the field (Genesis 39:5).

Here's the situation. Everything that Joseph touched prospered. It was as if he had the Midas touch, where everything he touched turned to gold. God wants us to have that same touch, that when the unsaved come into our presence, they can't stay the same. When situations seem hopeless for friends and loved ones, God will use us in such a way to restore what was lost. God wants to use us in such a way that those who hang around us are blessed because of us. That which we have will become contagious: our giving spirit, our forgiving spirit, and our humble spirit. People will not be able to stay away from you because they will understand that the best company for them to keep is with men and women, boys and girls who are living lives for Jesus Christ. They will see the benefits manifested not only in your life but also in the lives of everyone who comes in contact with you. What an awesome feeling to know God will use our lives to bless others! Isn't that what it is all about anyway? God always blesses those who He can send a blessing through. If you hog everything God sends you and never pass it on, you have a character flaw and it's called stinginess. Get rid of it. The next time you receive something you really like for yourself, give it away. Become a vessel that God can work through and you will be a person God will give to.

With Joseph around, Potiphar's house ran smoothly. Potiphar didn't worry about what was in his house; he trusted that Joseph would take care of everything. Joseph was not a burden to Potiphar, he was a blessing. Are there people around you that you just wish would go away because they do more harm than good? There is a name for these types of people; they are called liabilities.

Liabilities cause losses. Liabilities create indebtedness. In Joseph's case with Potiphar, all Joseph caused was blessing to come to the house of his master. Joseph was not a liability, Joseph was an asset. Assets bring increase. Assets create liberty. God is in search of people who will be assets in His kingdom and not liabilities. Assets cause things to grow while liabilities cause things to die. As children of God, we are in the growing business, helping people grow closer to God. If our character is of such that it causes people to grow away from God rather than to Him, we are liabilities to the kingdom. I don't know about you, but I want to be an asset and not a liability.

If you desire to be an asset to the kingdom of God, here are a few steps to take that will get you on the right road:

1. **Invest in the lives of others and God will invest in you.**
2. **Help someone fulfill their goal or vision and God will help you fulfill yours.**
3. **Use what you have now wisely and He will give you more.**
4. **Give thanks for all you have now even though it may not seem like much.**
5. **Consult Him in all things.**
6. **Give your best in all you do.**
7. **Don't be a grumbler.**
8. **Rejoice in the success of others.**

Finishers Wanted

When you are an asset, you can be counted on to get the job done.

So he left everything he owned in Joseph's charge; and with him there he did not concern himself with anything except the food, which he ate (Genesis 39:6).

It seems that Potiphar had confidence in Joseph that he would get the job done. The only thing Potiphar concerned himself with was what he ate. Everything else was left up to Joseph. The feeding of the livestock, the paying of bills, the handling of disputes.....whatever needed to be done in the house was left up to Joseph. You don't give this type of responsibility to people who only start things and never finish them. The church is full of starters, but not enough finishers. We start a lot of projects every year with the enthusiasm that "this is the year." We commit to seeing it through, but after a few months pass, the numbers grow thin and the same faithful few are left to carry the load the rest of the way. This has to stop. The church is not the place for people who only start races that others have to finish. An article in Quote magazine, July 1991 depicts the triumphant story of a Tanzanian runner.

Hours behind the runner in front of him, the last marathoner finally entered the stadium. By that time, the drama of the day's events was almost over and most of the spectators had gone home. This athlete's story, however, was still being played out.

Limping into the arena, the Tanzanian runner grimaced with every step, his knee bleeding and bandaged from an earlier fall. His ragged appearance immediately caught the attention of the remaining crowd, who cheered him on to the finish line.

Why did he stay in the race? What made him endure his injuries to the end? When asked these questions later, he replied, "My country did not send me 7,000 miles away to start the race. They sent me 7,000 miles to finish it."

Whenever you feel like quitting, remember there are angels all around cheering you on. Don't quit when it comes to the things of God. Yes, we fall down, get cut up, feelings are hurt, but inspite of all the obstacles, if you have the courage to begin, God will help you to finish. You may not be the most gifted, but it doesn't matter. It doesn't say the race is given to the most gifted, the race is given to those who endure, and those who finish will wear the crown. If you start something, finish it. If you make a vow, pay it. If you make a promise, uphold it. Be a finisher, and you will always be in demand!

Calvin Coolidge, the thirtieth president of the United States said, "We don't need more knowledge, we need more character!" I agree. With all our knowledge about the bible, we are walking with very little power. Knowledge alone will not save souls. Simply knowing about God is not enough. You must know Him and when you truly know Him your light will shine brightly giving light to all those in darkness.

Character will restrict you

And it came about after these events that his master's wife looked with desire at Joseph, and said, "Lie with me." But he refused and said to his master's wife, "Behold, with me here, my master does not concern himself with anything in the house, and he has put all that he owns in my charge. There is no one greater in this house than I, and he has withheld nothing from me except you, because you are his wife. How then could I do this great evil, and sin against God?" And it came about as she spoke to Joseph day after day, that he did not listen to her to lie beside her, or be with her (Genesis 39:7-10, NAS).

There are some things we just should not do. Some of us will say, will do, and will go anywhere, but when you have godly character, you are restricted as to what you do. Joseph could have easily said, "well I am just a man," and slept with Potiphar's wife but his character would not allow him to do so.

Can you imagine the predicament Joseph was in? Here this beautiful woman is making advances at him. She's an older woman and what a trophy this could be for him! We all are faced with these types of situations in life. They may not be sexual advances, but we are all faced with things and opportunities we know we have no business participating in. What do you do? What do you say? In these times our character takes the stand and speaks on our behalf, "I can, but I can't. I can but I can't because of who He is to me. No one may ever find out, but He will know and He matters most. I can't live knowing he knows." Yes, He knows all, He sees all, and He hears all. Nothing escapes His all-seeing eye. Character restricts you from doing those things you would normally do in your flesh. Character causes you to hold your tongue when you would normally go off. Character will make you say "no" to what you use to say "yes" to.

It is a shame that so many people in the church will do and say just about anything because they have no character. There are some things we as Christians just ought not to do. When you have godly character, it doesn't mean that you will not be tempted. It does not mean you will not have the desire to yield to the temptation; however, it does mean that when you try to make a move toward that forbidden fruit, your character will act as a leash and pull you back in. Pray to God to tighten the leash around your neck. Develop godly character in your life that will restrict you from doing those things that will bring shame to God's name.

I know many people in the body of Christ who have been blessed with wonderful gifts and talents; some singers, some preachers, some musicians, and so on. Often I have seen them ascribe to a certain level only to fall down again and again. I often ask the question "why isn't he or she at a greater level of responsibility? Why isn't this person doing more with what they have?" One morning I turned on the television to hear eleven of the most life changing words I have ever heard, *"Your gift will take you where your character can't keep you."*

These words were spoken by Joyce Meyer and how true they are. You can be the most gifted person in the world but without character, you won't last long. When we rely solely on our gifts, we fail every time. God is not impressed with our gifts because He is the one who gave them to us. Your gift doesn't impress Him at all. What He is concerned with is your character. Can He trust you to not exalt the gift above the Giver of the gift? Be careful not to get wrapped up in your gift because there is always someone better than you at what you do and the only thing that will distinguish you from the rest is your character. Can God trust you to remain faithful through adversity? Can he trust you to keep Him first when men are applauding you? Can He trust you to say no to the things your flesh yearns for you to say yes to?

This type of character can't be taught in a seminar. It can't be learned from a twelve-step manual. This type of character comes from a personal relationship with Jesus Christ and making Him Lord in your life. Step out on faith right now and ask God to create in you a desire to want to be a person of godly character and watch the windows of heaven open up over your life. What type of people are we to be? We are to be people of godly character who influence the world for Jesus Christ.

Chapter 9

Beyond Sunday Morning

And day by day continuing with one mind in the temple, and breaking bread from house to house, they were taking their meals together with gladness and sincerity of heart, praising God, and having favor with all the people. And the Lord was adding to their number day by day those who were being saved (Acts 2:46, 47 NAS).

The increase of the early church was the natural result of the spiritual make-up of the faith community. Through their unselfish love towards one another and their commitment to the cross and the resurrection of Jesus Christ, they became an example of the life and ministry of the Lord Jesus Christ. In this atmosphere it was common to sell possessions for the benefit of the body. It was common to forgive a wrong and restore the person back to his or her original state with no strings attached. The church was based on love and all who saw it were amazed. Simply by living what they believed, they were respected by all who came in contact with them to the point that we read they had *favor with all the people and the Lord was adding to their number day by day those who were being saved.*

We cannot expect these results from what we do on Sunday mornings. Sunday mornings are re-fueling stops for us to be re-energized to get back into the day-to-day race of living the Christian life. It's time to go beyond Sunday morning. Live as lights every day in this dark world. Love your brothers and sisters in Christ unconditionally and offer your best to God. We can do it. We must do it! If we want to see lives changed, we must change what we know is not working and what is hindering the work of the Holy Spirit. Let's pattern our personal lives and the life of the church after the lives and work of the early church.

We are living in a hurting world.   People are desperately searching for answers to difficult issues and are struggling to find joy and peace in a world full of chaos and disappointment.   The church must reflect the goodness of God through word and deed. Our lights must shine so brightly that the world will not only see the radiance, but they will also be compelled to walk toward the light and be led by the Light.   I pray that we will realize how important we are to the healing of our world.   With this final thought in mind, listen to 2 Kings 2:19-22.

Then the men of the city said to Elisha, "Behold now, the situation of the city is pleasant, as my lord sees; but the water is bad, and the land is unfruitful." And he said, "Bring me a new jar, and put salt in it." So they brought it to him.   And he went out to the spring of water, and threw salt in it and said, "Thus says the Lord, 'I have purified these waters; there shall not be from there death or unfruitfulness any longer,'" So the waters have been purified to this day, according to the word of Elisha which he spoke.

No more business as usual.

This is a new day!

Good morning.   Let's pray.

Dear Lord,

Thank you for showing me how important I am to the body of Christ.   I confess that I have caused the church harm as well as myself.   Forgive me for all the people I have caused to go astray. Forgive me for not being a finisher.   Forgive me for not placing You first in my life.   But right now Lord, I give to you all of me.   I want to be used by You anyway you see fit.   I will say what You want me to say; I will do what You want me to do.   I want to be a catalyst to restore the church back to its original intent.

Thank You for hearing and answering my prayer.   In Jesus name, Amen.

To order additional copies or for bookings, contact
People of Integrity Ministries
2115 Laurel Branch Way
Houston, Texas 77014
(281) 587-9459
walter71@sbcglobal.net

About the Author

Walter Gibson is the Minister of Christian Education at New Mt. Calvary Baptist Church in Houston, Texas. He is a graduate of Houston Graduate School of Theology and is highly respected as a speaker, motivator, and a man of integrity. Walter lives with his wife Tarsha and two children in Houston, Texas.

35161633R00078

Made in the USA
Lexington, KY
01 April 2019